TAHOE RIM TRAIL

TAHOE RIM TRAIL

**The Official Guide
for Hikers,
Mountain Bikers,
and Equestrians**

ENDORSED BY
THE TAHOE RIM
TRAIL ASSOCIATION

Tim Hauserman

 WILDERNESS PRESS · BERKELEY, CA

Tahoe Rim Trail: A Complete Guide for Hikers, Mountain Bikers, and Equestrians

1st EDITION June 2002
2nd EDITION August 2008

Front and back cover photos copyright © 2008 by Tahoe Rim Trail Association
Interior photos, except where noted, by Tim Hauserman
Animal print illustrations by Jessica Land; illustration of "Inconsiderate Backcountry
Blockhead" by Karen Schwartz
Maps: Tom Harrison, using mapping information from Jeffrey P. Schaffer
Cover design: Lisa Pletka
Book design: Linda Ronan
Book editor: Roslyn Bullas

ISBN 978-0-89997-472-9
UPC 7-19609-97472-7

Manufactured in the United States of America

Published by: Wilderness Press
               1345 8th Street
               Berkeley, CA 94710
               (800) 443-7227; FAX (510) 558-1696
               info@wildernesspress.com
               www.wildernesspress.com

Visit our website for a complete listing of our books and for ordering information.

Frontispiece: McCloud Falls, in Ward Canyon. Photo: Tim Hauserman

FSC
Recycled
Supporting responsible
use of forest resources

Cert no. SW-COC-002283
www.fsc.org
© 1996 Forest Stewardship Council

ACKNOWLEDGMENTS—2nd EDITION

In addition to all the help I received for the first edition, I would like to add my thanks to the "Tim's 2007 Solo TRT Thru Hike" Team. I walked out my door and around the Rim Trail in two weeks, but if it were not for the water deliveries by Kevin Murnane, Anne Greenwood, and Denese Pillsbury and the food drops brought to me by Jan Corda and Joe Pace, I would have died of thirst and hunger. So thanks, guys and gals. Once again, big kudos to the Tahoe Rim Trail Association. Special thanks to Hannah Hauserman for indexing. Finally, thanks to all those who read the first edition and came up with suggestions. I did not, however, take the recommendation to make the book small enough to carry in your backpack. Just buy two copies, and rip out the parts you need to take with you out of one.

ACKNOWLEDGMENTS—1st EDITION

First of all, I want to thank Mother Nature, whose handiwork in creating Lake Tahoe so impressed me with its beauty that I could not stay away. This book is the result of all the joy I have felt in the woods and meadows around Lake Tahoe.

The Tahoe Rim Trail Association has been supportive along the way, especially former Associate Director Shannon Raborn, who heard me say too many times, "Could you read through this and let me know what you think?" Sara Holm, who had the joy of reading it at different stages, let me know when it was improving. Thanks to all TRTA Board Members who also read sections of the book to make sure I was on the right track; these include Max Jones, Jay Abdo, Jennifer Hogler, Jim Backhus, Shirley Moore, and others. Lynda McDowell, Executive Director of the Tahoe Rim Trail, has also been supportive.

Thanks to Robert McDowell, David Allessio, and Lori Allessio at the Forest Service for many excellent suggestions. Shelly Segale

Islands await at Middle Velma Lake.

and Karen Honeywell reviewed the manuscript and also contributed useful comments. Susie Denison wrote a terrific local book, *The Dog Lover's Guide to Lake Tahoe*, and convinced me that I could write this one. She told me it would not be easy. She was right.

Thanks to my buddies who hiked and biked with me and put up with my blabbing into a tape recorder: Jan Corda, Monika Klecka (the over-the-bars champ), Bud Tremayne, Shannon Raborn, Toni Blair, Laurie Buffington, and Karen Schwartz. The Tahoe Rim Trail 150-Mile Club encouraged me to hike the trail the first time, which made it easier the second and the third. Tahoe Trips and Trails gave me the occasional thrill of getting paid to hike; they've got a great manual on animals and plants at Lake Tahoe. I am very appreciative that I have been allowed to use the wonderful animal print drawings by Jessica Land, a fellow guide at Tahoe Trips and Trails. Rick Galleen let me look through all the trail information that he has collected.

Thanks to Glenn Hampton for starting the trail in the first place. Tom Harrison's dog-eared map went with me on all my hikes and I thank him for creating the maps in this book. Thanks to all the great horse folks, including Sonya Willits, whose cogent letter summarized the horse issue for me, and to Clayton Myers, Bob Stevens, and Jim Larimer for their information on horse-back riding on the Rim Trail. My helpful fishing sources included Jerome Yesavage, Bruce Ajari, and Ralph Cutter. Anne Bryant from the Bear Preservation League reviewed my bear information and was a great source on squirrels.

Besides providing information and assistance, Jeffrey P. Schaffer, another Wilderness Press author, read and reviewed the manuscript in detail and contributed to the wonderful maps in the book. His reputation for meticulous mapping and guidebook authoring skills is well deserved.

My wife, Sandy, and daughters, Sarah and Hannah, had to hear too many times, "Sorry I can't make it, I will be out hiking that day." Thanks to local Tahoe City merchants like The Back Country and Alpenglow who told me the book would sell. Wilderness Press had faith in me. I still remember the first message on my voice mail: "We will do your book, but it will need a lot of editing." Yes, as my editor Jannie Dresser can attest, those words were oh so true. Speaking of Jannie, she stuck with me valiantly through many drafts, guiding the text to be as good as it could be.

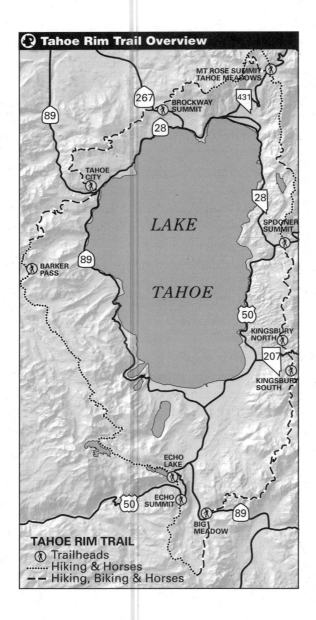

Tahoe Rim Trail Overview

89

267

BROCKWAY
SUMMIT

431

MT ROSE SUMMIT
TAHOE MEADOWS

28

TAHOE
CITY

28

SPOONER
SUMMIT

89

BARKER
PASS

LAKE

TAHOE

50

KINGSBURY
NORTH

207

KINGSBURY
SOUTH

ECHO
LAKE

50

ECHO
SUMMIT

BIG
MEADOW

89

TAHOE RIM TRAIL

Ⓧ Trailheads
.... Hiking & Horses
— — Hiking, Biking & Horses

Contents

A Note from the Tahoe Rim Trail Association

An organization and trail system born out of the passion and desire to create a memorable and life changing outdoor experience, the Tahoe Rim Trail Association (TRTA) has been built on years of dedicated volunteers, staff, agency partners, and community support. In 2006 the Tahoe Rim Trail Association celebrated 25 years as a nonprofit organization working hard with its partners to build and maintain a trail like no other…the Tahoe Rim Trail.

The Tahoe Rim Trail Association is grateful for support from a diverse group of outdoor enthusiasts who continue to support the organization with thousands of volunteer hours annually. Many volunteers offer their support as trail builders, trail maintainers, office assistants, and board members. The Tahoe Rim Trail Association's volunteer trail builders and maintainers, supported by the US Forest Service and Nevada State Parks, are responsible for the layout and design of the Tahoe Rim Trail. The Association's volunteers are also responsible for the trail construction and maintenance of the Tahoe Rim Trail.

Thousands of workers of all ages have staked, raked, pruned, hauled, sawn, shoveled, and pried in sun and snow, dust, and rain. Many have returned again and again and continue to do so, drawn by the camaraderie and high spirits of fellow volunteers and rewarded with a deep sense of pride in building and maintaining this magnificent public resource as their legacy. Today we continue to work with our volunteer supporters and agency partners to maintain and enhance this trail system in the Sierra Nevada.

Tim Hauserman's guidebook serves as a wonderful tool for those interested in dayhikes, backpacking trips, mountain bike rides, runs, horseback rides, and more. We hope you will use this guide when planning your adventure in the Sierra Nevada overlooking what Mark Twain called "the Jewel of the Sierra," Lake Tahoe.

We invite you to join the famous TRTA 165 Mile Club upon completion of all 8 segments of the Tahoe Rim Trail. Whether

Fontanillis Lake and Dicks Peak

you hike it in ten days or ten years, anyone who completes the trail is welcome in this club. Upon completion of the trail you will be asked to fill out a simple form documenting your journey. When we receive your form, the TRTA will assign you a 165 Mile Club member number and send a certificate, pin, and patch.

The TRTA also depends on the support of our many donors and members in ensuring the success of the organization. All TRTA members receive quarterly newsletters with updates on trail programs and the Association, invitations to all TRTA events, including the Annual Meeting, and an opportunity to join the 165 Mile Club. We invite you to become a member and join the family of friends who continue to support the legacy created by thousands to benefit millions for generations to come. More information on the Tahoe Rim Trail and the Association can be found at www.tahoerimtrail.org.

Mark Kimbrough, Executive Director,
Tahoe Rim Trail Association, Summer 2008

Foreword

As a cool dawn breaks high atop Mt. Tallac, I find myself completely spellbound by the spectacular awe-inspiring panorama before me. And my Impossible Dream of a trail completely around Lake Tahoe on the highest and most prominent mountain slopes suddenly takes shape.

Imagine a trail that winds completely around the most spectacular lake in the United States. As you hike along the 165-mile loop, you meander through areas rich in history. The trail leads you through old Washoe hunting grounds and long-vanished game trails, as well as trails made by early settlers fresh from obtaining their provisions at Genoa. Here, over 100 years ago, some of the West's first Basque sheepherders roamed through the mountain meadows with their flocks. You wade through waist-high grass, through magnificent stands of red fir and Jeffrey pine, and alongside cool mountain streams. You may journey high above mysterious places with names like "Hellhole" with its many pools and ground that shakes, rolls, and sways. At Grass Lake, you skirt the largest bog in the Sierra Nevada, while most of the time you can view the highest and largest alpine lake in North America, Lake Tahoe. On the horizon, you can make out the Pine Nut Range in Nevada, the Sierra of California and the Carson Valley. You travel through six counties, three National Forests, and two states. A week and a half later, you're back where you started. This was the dream that inspired the Tahoe Rim Trail nearly twenty years ago.

Today, thanks to over 10,000 volunteers who worked tirelessly for over 18 years, the Tahoe Rim Trail has become a reality. In September of 2001, it officially opened with a ceremony that marked the completion of the last section of the trail. Now, you can enjoy this challenging trail by using Tim Hauserman's excellent guide with its concise and accurate descriptions of the fascinating vegetation that blankets the area. You will also be introduced to the many animals you may encounter along the trail. The maps, produced by Tom Harrison, and mileage figures, verified by Jeffrey P. Schaffer, will help you better plan a safe and enjoyable trip. This guide will fast become your constant companion on the trail.

Use this guide to increase your awareness for the proper use and respect for the resources of the Tahoe Basin, but also use it to fully enjoy our new national treasure, the Tahoe Rim Trail.

Glenn Hampton
Founder of the Tahoe Rim Trail, May 2002

Sunrise from viewpoint near Martis Peak

Showers Lake

Dicks Lake from Dicks Pass

Mountain bikes between Tahoe Meadows and Tunnel Creek

1

Introduction to the Tahoe Area and the Tahoe Rim Trail

Then it seemed to me the Sierra should not be called the Nevada, or Snowy Range, but the Range of Light. And after ten years spent in the heart of it, rejoicing and wondering, bathing in its glorious floods of light, seeing the sunbursts of morning among the icy peaks, the noonday radiance on the trees and rocks and snow, the flush of the alpenglow, and a thousand dashing waterfalls with their marvelous abundance of irised spray, it still seems to be above all others the Range of Light, the most divinely beautiful of all the mountain chains I have ever seen.
—John Muir, 1912

Welcome to the Tahoe Rim Trail! This book will quickly and easily provide you with what you need to know in order to enjoy your time on this incredibly beautiful route. Having lived at Lake Tahoe most of my life, I've spent countless hours on area trails. While I am not a biologist, a geologist, a naturalist, or an "ist" of any kind, I have learned enough about Tahoe plants, animals, and mountains to deepen my interest when I am in the woods. I'd like to help make your outdoor experience just as fun and fascinating.

An enormous, deep-blue, subalpine lake surrounded by lofty, snowcapped peaks. Lush, green forests, dark volcanic peaks, stark granite faces and hundreds of small, jewel-like lakes adorning the wilderness areas above this special lake. Should someone build a loop trail here? Absolutely! In fact it is quite remarkable that the trail was completed as recently as September 2001. If a loop trail should have been built anywhere in the world, this was the place.

The now 165-mile Tahoe Rim Trail (or TRT, as it is sometimes abbreviated here) circles one of the world's most beautiful lakes, and winds through two states, several wilderness areas, National Forest and state park lands, and an incredible diversity of geology, flora, and fauna. The trail accesses both the Sierra Nevada and its Carson Range spur, each with a unique personality. It winds through aspen meadows, skirts high mountain peaks, and runs for miles along ridgetops with stunning views. You can walk for miles under a forested canopy, or saunter through meadows. You can venture above treeline for long stretches. That the trail is a big loop, a circle, may be its best feature. Wherever you set off, as the days and weeks go by, you can follow the circle back to where you began. Across the big, blue expanse of the lake, you can pick out where you were a week ago, and where you will be again in another week. A multi-use path, much of the Tahoe Rim Trail was constructed for the pleasure of hikers, equestrians, and mountain bikers, using modern trail-building techniques, with the goal to not exceed an average grade of 10 percent.

Geographic Setting

Lake Tahoe is the largest subalpine lake in North America. At 22 miles long and 12 miles wide it is a beautiful expanse of deep, blue water. What makes it so intensely blue? The depth. At its deepest point Lake Tahoe plunges to 1645 feet with an average depth of approximately 900 feet. With its huge surface area, that's a lot of water. Tahoe is blue also because it is so clear and clean. The clarity is primarily due to the fact that the basin around the lake is fairly small, the water very cold, and the soils and vegetation have prevented nutrients from entering the lake where they increase algae growth.

Since the 1960s and 1970s there has been dramatic population growth and increased development in the Tahoe area.

Development has had a negative impact on the lake. An increase in algae growth has reduced Tahoe's legendary clarity. A substantial investment of energy and money is now underway to protect the lake. For more information on how you can help, contact the League to Save Lake Tahoe at (530) 541-5388 or the Tahoe Regional Planning Agency at (775) 588-4547. Call or write your Congressperson or Senator to ask for their support in efforts to clean up and protect this lake and its surroundings. You will find a handy list of "Ways to Save Lake Tahoe" at the end of this book.

Trail History

Glenn Hampton was a Recreation Officer for the Lake Tahoe Basin Management Unit of the United States Forest Service through the 1970s when he first had the idea of completing a trail with volunteer labor around the rim of Lake Tahoe. He forged a partnership between the Forest Service, the Nevada State Parks, and a newly created, not-for-profit volunteer organization called the Tahoe Rim Trail Fund. The purpose of the partnership was to plan, construct, and maintain a Tahoe Rim Trail. Since 1984 more than 100 miles of trail have been built or improved around the lake. The Tahoe Rim Trail also uses the existing Pacific Crest Trail in the section that overlaps from Meiss Meadows to Twin Peaks.

The Tahoe Rim Trail Fund (now known as the Tahoe Rim Trail Association) is administered by a volunteer Board of Directors and has a small professional staff. The trail has been built partially by professional crews hired by the Forest Service or Nevada State Parks, and partially by volunteers who have contributed thousands of hours. For many it has been a labor of love. Construction of the trail began in July 1984 from Grass Lake, on the north side of Highway 89 near Luther Pass, toward Kingsbury Grade. In 1985 two additional construction projects were started at Spooner Summit and Tahoe City. In 2001 the last section of the trail was completed, between Rose Knob Peak and Mount Baldy.

View from Dicks Pass

In 1999 then First Lady, Hillary Rodham Clinton and the White House Millennium Council designated the Tahoe Rim Trail as the Millennium Trail for the State of Nevada. Bestowed on only one trail in each state, the Tahoe Rim Trail is certainly worthy of this honor and is destined to become one of the most popular trails in the United States, taking its place beside the Appalachian Trail, the Pacific Crest Trail, and the John Muir Trail.

The Tahoe Rim Trail Association

Funded through contributions, memberships, fundraising, and the sale of merchandise, the Tahoe Rim Trail Association has arranged for some 10,000 volunteers to work over 200,000 hours on the trail. The TRTA and their government partners have not only built or improved the trail, but they have also built two major trailhead facilities, and a 1.3-mile wheelchair-accessible interpretive trail. The TRTA is the prime information source for people interested in hiking, biking, or horseback riding on the Tahoe Rim Trail.

The TRTA also administers the Tahoe Rim Trail 165-Mile Club. Those who hike or bike (where allowed) the entire trail can become members of the Tahoe Rim Trail 165-Mile Club.

Even though the Tahoe Rim Trail was completed in 2001, there is still much to do in order to maintain and improve the trail. Tasks include repairing damaged sections of the trail, as well as making changes to the trail to prevent future damage. Volunteers continue to add switchbacks, change routes, add connecting trails, and do whatever is necessary to improve the trail.

The Tahoe Rim Trail Association is key to the future of the trail and anyone can become a member. Members receive quarterly newsletters, an invitation to the annual meeting, discounts on merchandise, the opportunity to attend TRTA-led hikes, horseback rides, and bike rides, not to mention the satisfaction of knowing that they are doing their part for this wonderful trail. To obtain information contact:

Tahoe Rim Trail Association
DWR Community Non-Profit Center
948 Incline Way
Incline Village, NV 89451
(775) 298-0012
info@tahoerimtrail.org
www.tahoerimtrail.org

Regulations and Permits

The Tahoe Rim Trail travels through three National Forest Wilderness Areas: Mt. Rose Wilderness, Desolation Wilderness, and Granite Chief Wilderness. Much of the rest of the trail is on National Forest lands in California and Nevada. The remainder of the trail lies in the Lake Tahoe Nevada State Park. The only areas with limitations on hiking or camping on the TRT are Desolation Wilderness and Lake Tahoe Nevada State Park. These include the following trail sections, described in greater detail in chapter 6.

Section 3: Tahoe Meadows to Spooner Summit. This section travels through Lake Tahoe Nevada State Park where camping is limited to two primitive but developed campgrounds which have picnic tables and pit toilets, but no water supplies. (The TRTA has provided bottled water at the Marlette Campground. Contact the TRTA to see if water is still currently available.) No permits are required here. For more information contact the Lake Tahoe Nevada State Park at (775) 831-0494 or the Tahoe Rim Trail Association office at (775) 298-0012.

Section 7: Echo Summit/Echo Lakes to Barker Pass. This section travels through Desolation Wilderness. Permits are required to enter Desolation Wilderness, and these permits can be obtained at the trailhead. If you are staying overnight, a camping permit must be obtained at the Tahoe Basin National Forest Information Center at Taylor Creek located on Highway 89 about 0.5 mile northwest of Camp Richardson. The wilderness has been divided into zones for the issuance of permits. A limited number of camping permits are available for each zone, so the possibility exists of not being able to obtain a permit for the more popular areas (which tend to be lakes close to trailheads) in the middle of the summer, particularly on weekends. For more information contact the Forest Service at:

Lake Tahoe Basin Management Unit
35 College Drive
South Lake Tahoe, CA 96150
(530) 543-2600
www.fs.fed.us/r5/ltbmu

2 Animals and Plants, Great and Small

The Lake Tahoe area has a tremendous variety of interesting flora and fauna. You will enhance your enjoyment and experience of this beautiful region by getting to know some of the animals and plants. This chapter gives a quick summary of what you may encounter as you journey along the Tahoe Rim Trail.

While many of these animals are a rare treat to encounter, the smaller animals such as squirrels and birds are found in abundance. Among the highlights of traveling in the Tahoe woods are the fascinating trees and wildflowers that you pass along the way. The descriptions of plants are designed to be simple to read and understand. This book provides a quick introduction to the most common animals and plants in the Tahoe Basin area; it is not intended to substitute for a good field guide. For those who want more information, several wildflower and plant field books are listed in the "Recommended Reading" section at the back of the book.

The Largest Animals in the Tahoe Region

Bear—The largest omnivores in the Sierra are black bears, but often their fur is cinnamon brown, dark brown, reddish and sometimes even off-white. Bears are common on the west shore of the lake, where numerous garbage cans provide a tempting place to scavenge a free meal on garbage collection days. Whether you live in the Tahoe area or are just visiting, you can do your part to protect bears—and yourself—by keeping your garbage away from where bears can get to it. If you are camping or backpacking in bear country, follow these simple rules:

- Don't leave any food or clothes that smell like food in your tent. When they come to get it, you don't want to be sleeping in the path of a hungry and determined bear.
- Put your food (all your food!) in a safe place at night and when you are not in camp. If a campground has a bearproof container use it. In the backcountry you are not only advised to put your food in a bearproof canister; in some areas, including several wilderness areas in the central and southern Sierra, you are required to do so. The next two best methods are to hang your food high in a tree, suspended from a rope, or to put it on a 15-foot-high rocky ledge where bears can't reach.

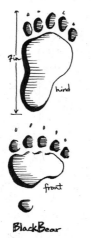

- Keep a clean camp so that bears or other animals won't be attracted to the site. Put food, cleaning and fragrant hygiene supplies such as shampoo, toothpaste, and soap away soon after you are done with them.
- If you see a bear, make lots of noise: bang pots and pans together, stand up and shout, and throw your arms around to scare the bear away. (Note: this doesn't always work!)
- Be smart. If a bear is chomping down on your food, it has already won, so don't try to take the food away from it.
- Never get between a mother bear and her cub.
- If you startle a bear, make eye contact, but do not stare at it. Instead, slowly back away and wait for the bear to amble off. Be sure to not block its escape route.
- Don't forget that bears are good runners and can climb trees.
- Treat bears with respect: remember, you are in their territory.

While it is important to be cautious, bear attacks are extremely rare. In those very unusual circumstances where bears have injured people, it was usually the result of human error. Be careful and enjoy bears from a safe distance.

Deer—The most common deer in the Sierra are named "mule deer" for their large, floppy ears that resemble those of a mule. Mule deer also sport a small white bob of a tail. Deep snow and lack of forage keep mule deer away from the area during winter months. At that time, you are more likely to find them in the warmer climes of the Carson Valley, a short jaunt over the Carson Range from the east shore. As the season warms up, these animals are commonly spotted on the east slopes and in other areas of the Tahoe basin.

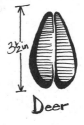

Mountain Lion or Cougar—Known as either a mountain lion or cougar, the rare and elusive mountain lion has been seen occasionally in the Tahoe area, especially in lower elevation open areas such as the east shore and around Truckee. These large cats range in size between 6.5 to 8 feet long, including tail, and can weigh up to 200 pounds. Each animal has a vast range and can cover many miles of territory in one night. Mountain lions hunt deer primarily, although they also prey on raccoons, birds, mice, and even skunks and porcupines. Porcupine?! That would have to be one hungry mountain lion.

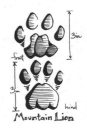

Someone once brought a pet mountain lion to my office: its power and grace were awe-inspiring. You had the feeling that it could dispose of any one of us in half a minute. Mountain lions can jump 12 feet up a tree from a standstill position. If you do encounter one, experts warn not to run. Instead try to look as big as possible by standing tall, opening up your jacket, and waving your arms. Once the cat perceives that you don't behave like prey, it will probably back off. Also, a mountain lion leaves the remains of a kill and returns later to eat; needless to say, it is not wise to hang around a lion kill.

Medium-Sized Animals

Bobcat—You are more likely to hear this elusive member of the cat family with its loud scream or howl than see it. With an average

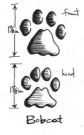

weight of about 20 pounds in adulthood, it is just a little larger than an average-sized domestic cat. A bobcat has a short stubby tail that is black toward the end and tipped with white. A nocturnal predator, the bobcat likes to dine on squirrels and mice. Bobcats have been rarely sighted in Tahoe Meadows, above Tahoe City, and along the west shore.

Coyote—These adaptable creatures are common in the Tahoe area. While I've seen them in many locations, they seem to prefer wood-

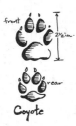

lands and meadows. They can often be heard yipping and howling at night in Ward and Blackwood canyons, Squaw Valley, Alpine Meadows, and other places. Though coyotes resemble medium-sized dogs, they are much more graceful and lissome when they run, a sight to behold. It is not uncommon for a dog to chase a single coyote, only to discover that the coyote is leading him back to his teammates. Although many believe that coyotes do not hunt in packs, I have seen them several times in groups of three or four adults. If you live in the mountains, take care with your domesticated animals, even around your home. Many a lost cat or small dog has become a coyote dinner.

Marten—It is a rare treat to spot a marten, also called pine marten. At about 1.5 to 3 feet long, including its tail, the marten is about the size of a housecat but longer and sleeker. Martens have beautiful lush brown fur and long bushy tails. They are agile climbers and sometimes live in a cavity high up in a tree. They are elusive animals, but can occasionally be seen in pursuit of squirrels or chipmunks, their favorite dinner. Several years ago we saw one in nearby trees around our Tahoe area house for about two weeks. The grace and stealth of the marten is unmatched.

Marmot—If you hear a high-pitched squeak when you are walking by a big rock pile, there is a good chance that it harbors a yellow-bellied marmot. Also known as woodchuck, the marmot is about the size of a house-cat. Related to squirrels, marmots are dark brown and cinnamon in color,

Marmot

live in groups and love to sun themselves on rocks. I have often seen them in Desolation Wilderness, on the Pacific Crest Trail near Twin Peaks, and in the Mt. Rose area.

Porcupine—These large rodents can often be seen on roads or sitting up in a tree. About 2 to 3 feet long, they are large and round with short legs. They have light brown to yellowish fur and numerous hollow but sharp quills of up to 3 inches long. The porcupine walks in a slow lumbering fashion—if no one wants to eat you, why hurry?—and enjoys a diet of succulent bark and herbaceous plants. No animals, except cougars perhaps, want to have anything to do with these quill-covered critters, and although the quills can cause a great deal of pain, especially to over-zealous dogs, it is a myth that they can "shoot" their quills.

Raccoon—These carnivorous little burglars are one of the most interesting animal species in the Sierra. The distinctive face looks

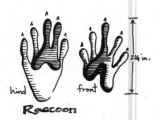

like a burglar's mask, with a black band across the eyes and most of the face white. They range in size, but can get as big as a medium-sized dog. Raccoons are nocturnal, all the better to wake you in the middle of the night while they are knocking over garbage cans in pursuit of food. It is common to see them on house decks but rare to see them in the wild. Often the best evidence of a raccoon is the very distinctive hand-like tracks they leave.

Small Animals

These ubiquitous rodents inhabit the ground, the trees, perhaps even your attic, and represent a fair percentage of local roadkill. A recent squirrel census reported 178 million squirrels in the Tahoe basin.

California Ground Squirrel—These squirrels have large bodies like the gray squirrels but have much smaller tails. They have a mottled brown coat and a silver saddle over the shoulder. They spend most of their time on the ground and are very busy all summer getting fattened up to hibernate through the winter.

Chickaree or Douglas Squirrel—This medium-sized dark brown squirrel has a reddish tinge on its back, a white belly, and a bushy tail with a silver tip. Chickarees stay active all winter and make a short explosive *quer-o* sound.

If you hear fir cones crashing down to the ground, and see the mangled remains of the soft cones sitting on a stump, you will know you are in chickaree country. These squirrels love to climb trees and drop the cones for later, when they remove the entire cone, piece by piece, in order to get to the tasty seeds inside.

Golden-mantled Ground Squirrel and Chipmunk—What is the difference between a chipmunk and the golden-mantled ground squirrel? A chipmunk is smaller, and has lines on its back that go all the way over its head. The Tahoe area's most common squirrel, the golden-mantled, has a lovely

Golden-mantled ground squirrel

white band bordered by black running up each side of its back and ending at its shoulders. Both species eat seeds, grasses, and fruit.

Western Flying Squirrel—These small brown squirrels (smaller than a chickaree) are very friendly and social, but since they are nocturnal most people will not have the opportunity to see one. They actually glide through the air from tree branch to branch. Like the Western gray squirrel, the flying squirrel remains active all winter.

Western Gray Squirrel—Larger than either the chickaree or ground squirrel, the gray squirrel also lives in the area but in smaller numbers. It has a uniform gray body and a long, broad tail. Like the chickaree, and unlike the ground squirrels and chipmunks, the gray squirrel is active all winter. It loves to sit in trees and "laugh" at cats and dogs, which stare at it with evil intent.

Pika or Cony—The pika is smaller than a chipmunk, light brown in color, and lives primarily in high rocky areas. It looks like a cross between a chipmunk and a small rabbit (and is in the same animal order as the latter) with shorter ears. It makes a peeping noise.

Birds

American Robin—Slightly smaller than the Steller's jay, the robin has a similar physique and is a frequent summer visitor to

Lake Tahoe. With its brick-red breast, yellow bill, and gray back, the robin cheerily hops through the understory of local woods or meadows, looking for insects or worms.

Bald Eagle—A very large, majestic black bird with white head, the bald eagle occasionally is spotted flying near water, perched on a large tree, or riding the updrafts. I remember watching an eagle fly along the lakeshore, when suddenly two ospreys began to chase it; the three completed some incredible acrobatic stunts before the ospreys gave up. Perhaps the eagle had ventured too near the osprey nest. Count yourself lucky if you see one of these rarer raptors.

Mountain Bluebird—A rare and beautiful treat, the mountain bluebird is a sky blue and startling in its soft beauty. About the size of a robin, it is a lighter blue than the much more common Steller's jay. Look for it in grassy meadows or at the edge of forest hunting insects. I have seen it in Ward Canyon and near Truckee.

Blue Grouse—You are more likely to hear a blue grouse than to see one. Males vocalize a very low, bass-drum *brrrmmmmmm, brrrmmmmm, brrrmmmmm* sound. Females are large, plump birds about the size of a pheasant or chicken. Their plumage is brownish gray with some white feathers near the neck. They can sometimes be seen in trees or brush. Breaking cover, they startle you as they suddenly take flight with a loud *wap, wap, wap* of wings. This bird can commonly be seen or heard in heavily wooded sections on the west shore, including Desolation Wilderness and areas north of Tahoe City.

Canada Goose—Commonly seen along Tahoe beaches and in parks, this large grayish-tan goose has a black head and neck, and a prominent white chin. Though geese are known to steal food from unsuspecting small children, they are beautiful when flying in their A-line formations. Less beautiful are the copious amounts of droppings they leave, making a trip to many a Tahoe beach akin to walking through the room of a teenager (messy but not dangerous).

Clark's Nutcracker—With a shape and sound similar to the Steller's jay, this light gray bird has black wings with white patches. Seen at treeline along high ridgetops, very much Tahoe Rim Trail country, Clark nutcrackers make a loud and slow *flap, flap, flap* with its wings as it flies from tree to tree. It prefers whitebark pines; a single bird can bury thousands of pine seeds in a summer season.

Mountain Chickadee—Perhaps the most common bird in the Tahoe woods, the small chickadee (about 5 inches long) is light gray with a black cap and white line over each eye. Usually quiet, this active bird may be best known for its call, which many people say sounds like *cheese, burrr, gerrrr*; others claim its call sounds more like *tsick-a-dee-dee-dee*. You be the judge. Maybe it just sounds like the voice of a chickadee.

Mountain Quail—California's state bird is small to medium-sized and slightly chunky. You can identify it by the little standard issuing from the top of its head, its gray to brown coloring, and the way it scurries away into nearby brush. It stays close to the ground under bushes near sunny open areas and water sources. Since quail convene in coveys, once you spot one, you will likely hear and see others.

Osprey—Another rare bird, the osprey is best known for its ability to swoop down and catch fish in its talons. The osprey is a little smaller than an eagle, with brown feathers on its back and white feathers on its breast. When flying above you, it appears mostly white, but while sitting in a nest with wings tucked, it can appear mostly brown. The osprey makes a high-pitched squeak and can

Twin Peaks from north of Tahoe City

be seen along the lakeshore or high up in large nests it has built out of sticks at the top of dead trees. I have watched an osprey dive into Dick's Lake and remove fish that were feeding in the evening.

Owl—Various species of owl inhabit the Tahoe area. Primarily nocturnal, they live in the deep woods and are more likely to be heard than seen. While the calls of owls vary with the species, in general you can hear a deep *who, who, who.* Owls have large, round faces with piercing front-facing eyes perfect for late night hunting. Some species have catlike ear tufts that stick straight up.

Steller's Jay—The seemingly ubiquitous Steller's jay is most often found at lake-level elevations and in campgrounds. It is medium-size with a dark blue body and a mantle, throat and crest that are black. Its aggressive raucous cry or squawk is distinctive. It will eat your potato chips and raid your snack packs, yet many Eastern birders delight in seeing this bird for the first time.

Western Tanager—Though somewhat uncommon, the tanager is one of the most colorful birds in the Tahoe area. The male has a red head, a bright yellow body, and black wings. The female is also bright yellow, but lacks the red head. Try to spot this small- to medium-sized bird (bigger than a chickadee, smaller than a Steller's jay) flitting from tree to tree.

Amphibians and Reptiles

Pacific Tree Frog—These tiny frogs can be heard in many Sierra locales. They are especially common in the grassy area around Twin Lakes, so if you're walking to these lakes be careful not to step on them. About 1 inch long, the frogs are brown or green with black eye stripes. Though called tree frogs, they have no special preference for trees and are just as comfortable on the ground or in the grass.

Snakes—Several snakes live in the Tahoe area. Happily for area hikers, the *rattlesnake* is not common among them. The most common snake in the Tahoe area is the *garter snake*. It is about 2 feet long or less, slender with a tail tapered to a sharp tip. The garter snake has a black or gray upper surface with a yellow line along its back. While for the most part it is harmless, if handled it may discharge a foul-smelling liquid. Less common to this area is the *rubber boa*. A wonder to behold, this docile, harmless small brown snake is usually less than 2 feet long. With its smooth skin, it looks like a worm on steroids.

Western Fence Lizard—This 6 to 9 inch lizard is often found in dry areas lounging on a rock or running to escape your big feet. The scaly skin of the lizard is gray and they are often seen doing little "push-ups" on the rocks, exposing their blue bellies.

Insects

Bees, Yellow Jackets, and Wasps—Honeybees and bumblebees quietly go about their business of pollinating flowers and rarely sting people. Yellow jackets, even though they look like a bee, are actually a form of wasp. After an above-average winter snowfall, especially in a season with a lot of spring moisture and cold temperatures, yellow jackets are found in small numbers. In drought conditions, however, yellow jackets multiply, and by late summer and fall they can be a nuisance. They are ferocious predators and meat-eaters and their stings can be painful and cause swelling. These wasps can nest in the ground or in a trailside log. If you get too close to their nests, they will come out in force to sting you. Wasps are most active from midday to just after sunset.

Mosquitoes—These pesky little critters can be a problem from mid-June through mid-July throughout the Tahoe area. The timing of their emergence from the shadows of spring, however, depends on the quantity of precipitation that arrived during winter and how quickly the snowpack melts. Mosquitoes are active at dusk and dawn and are prevalent in shady forest areas, as well as in and near meadows, along a lakeshore, near creeks and any body of standing water or moist area. They especially like small, shallow bodies of water where they breed. To avoid mosquitoes, either pack a lot of insect repellent, take to a granite mountain or ridgetop area, or pray for wind.

Fish

Fish have not been seen recently on the Tahoe Rim Trail, but there are some in the streams and lakes that you might pass. Here are the few to look out for:

Brook Trout—Not a true trout, but a char, its lighter colored spots on a dark green-gray background distinguish the brook. It also has a yellow- to ruddy-colored underbelly. It can be found in any Sierra water source.

Brown Trout—Hugging river bottoms, the brown trout sports an olive green to cinnamon brown coloring with reddish spots along their sides. These fish were imported into the Sierra from Germany and Scotland.

Cutthroat Trout—The most common fish in the mountain lakes and streams, the cutthroat can be identified by its red, orange or yellow "slash" marks under each jaw. It is sometimes called the spotted trout.

Mackinaw or Lake Trout—Incorrectly blamed for eliminating the cutthroat from Lake Tahoe, the Mackinaw trout is also a char family member like the brooky mentioned above. It is the least colorful of all the Sierra fish, gray with some yellow speckles that brighten during spawning season. It grows to a large size; every year 20- to 30-pound mackinaws are caught in Lake Tahoe and Donner Lake, and 10-pound fish are common.

Rainbow Trout—With a bluish-gray to gray-green back, silvery belly, and dark black speckles, the rainbow's most distinctive mark is a red streak down each side. Mountain men and prospectors introduced rainbows into the Sierra in the 1800s.

Kokanee Salmon—Introduced in the 1940s into the Tahoe area lakes, the Kokanee can be found here still. It has a robust body and dusky, olive to bluish coloring. It is silvery on its underside and nests in bottom gravel like the rainbow trout. During their fall spawning run, they turn bright red and can be found in large numbers in Taylor Creek, on Lake Tahoe's South Shore. Sometimes they are also found in smaller numbers spawning up Eagle Creek, right next to the Vikingsholm Castle near Emerald Bay.

Trees

White Fir—Probably the most common tree in the Tahoe Basin, white fir typically grows below 6500 feet in elevation (although they are sometimes seen up to 7500 feet). They have gray bark and short, bunched needles that have an average length of 1.5 to 2 inches and a flat appearance. The bark of younger trees is somewhat smooth; as the trees age, the bark gets rougher and more like that of other pine and fir trees. The light green upright cones are soft and found scattered about the woods—the work of chickarees. During the drought of the early 1990s, these firs died in extensive numbers after an insufficient water supply made them vulnerable to disease and beetle infestations.

Red Fir—White firs' red cousin dominates the landscape in some areas above 6500 feet, often living in dense stands. The red fir needle bunches are tighter than those of the white fir, curve inward, and grow to over an inch long. The bark is reddish-brown to gray and the tree sprouts mid-sized cones of 6 to 9 inches as compared to the shorter ones of white fir (3 to 5 inches).

Jeffrey Pine—Jeffrey pine is the dominant pine tree in much of the Tahoe Sierra and, though it is especially prevalent near lake level, it can grow at elevations up to 8000 feet. Jeffrey pine can reach a height of 180 feet. It has thick gray to reddish bark, which turns redder as the tree matures, and smells like butterscotch, vanilla or pineapple depending on what kind of nose you have. It also has large roundish cones with up-turning prickles and long needles of three.

Ponderosa or Western Yellow Pine—Similar to the Jeffrey, the ponderosa prefers lower elevations, usually below 6500 feet. and grows in smaller numbers near Lake Tahoe. It has yellowish to reddish-brown bark and often reaches heights of 100 feet. Like Jeffrey pine, ponderosa also has long needles of three. Ponderosa pine cone prickles stick up and out, while the Jeffrey's turn up and in (remember "gentle Jeffrey" or "prickly ponderosa"). In some areas, a hybridized combination of Jeffrey and ponderosa is found, making identification difficult.

Lodgepole Pine—This usually straight tree (hence its value as a lodge pole for Native Americans) is very common in a variety of soil conditions from below 6000 feet to over 9000 feet in elevation. It has thin, scaly, light gray and sappy bark, and small cones. The needles are in bunches of two and can be made into an "L" for lodgepole. The tree prefers wet areas and its presence often signals mosquito territory.

Sugar Pine—These beautiful, majestic trees can reach a height of 250 feet. They are uncommon above 6500 feet and rare in lower elevations since most were cut down for lumber at the end of the 19th century. Sugar pine has long cylindrical cones that grow 10 to 16 inches downward from the tips of long graceful branches. John Muir said of the sugar pine that it "is the noblest pine yet discovered, surpassing all others not merely in size but also in kingly beauty and majesty."

Western White Pine—These trees grow at higher elevations of 7000 feet to 9000 feet and can reach 150 feet in height although they are usually much smaller because of the harsh conditions in which they live. Like the whitebark pine, the western white pine has needles that come in clusters of five. Its cone resembles that of the sugar pine though it is shorter (6 to 8 inches) and narrower. The upper

Tree Altitude Chart

Trees in the Sierra tend to find their niche at a particular altitude. By knowing your altitude, you might be able to identify the tree, and if you know the tree it might help you determine the altitude. The one exception to the rule is the lodgepole pine, which seems to be found at nearly any mountain elevation. The chart below details where trees are dominant. Be aware that you may find a few stragglers above and below the listed ranges. But if, for example, you see lots of western white pines and no sugar pines, you will know that you are above 7000 feet in elevation.

6000-6500 feet White fir, Jeffrey pine, ponderosa pine, sugar pine, lodgepole, aspen, incense cedar

6500-7000 feet Red fir, Jeffrey pine, lodgepole, aspen

7000-8000 feet Hemlock, western white pine, red fir, mountain juniper, lodgepole

8000-9000 feet Hemlock, western white pine, juniper, lodgepole, whitebark pine

Above 9000 feet Whitebark pine

branches of a western white pine, also known as silver pine, turn upward at their tips. Mature trees have a distinctive checkerboard pattern on their bark.

Whitebark Pine—This high elevation tree is usually found near mountaintops and is easily mistaken for a lodgepole pine. The tree has short stiff needles clustered in groups of five (while the lodgepole needles are in groups of two). The bark is gray-white, and the cones are small and dark brown. It is also common to see them near the tops of peaks in a shrub-like formation called *krummholz* where they may only stand a foot or so high.

Aspen or Quaking Aspen—The Sierra's most colorful deciduous tree derives its name from the appearance it has when its leaves "quake" in gentle breezes or wind storms. With white bark and oval-shaped leaves, aspens are common in wet and moist areas, along creek beds, near springs, and in meadows. Their presence can indicate a ground-water source. Aspen trees throw out "shooters" of smaller trees, which grow up around the base of their trunks; a single tree may put out dozens of shooters and thus a whole grove may have started with one tree. This tree provides most of the fall yellow and gold color.

Cedar tree close to Tahoe City

Incense Cedar—These trees can grow to a height of 150 feet. Incense cedar is commonly found near the lake (6200 feet) with an upper elevation of around 6500 feet, a little higher in sunny locations. Incense cedars have red to cinnamon-brown flaky bark, and dark green short needles, which lie in flat feathery groupings.

Mountain Hemlock—Mountain hemlock prefers high snow areas above 7000 feet and are common above 8000 feet in many north-facing areas along the Tahoe Rim Trail, generally in areas of maximum snowpack. A beautiful and majestic tree reaching heights of 25 to 100 feet, with smaller trees at the highest elevations, mountain hemlock has short dark green needles that grow on branches that cover the tree from bottom to top. The branches have a gentle sloping appearance; the cones are small and dark brown. What makes the mountain hemlock especially magical is the way the top of the tree droops over like a wizard's hat.

Western (Sierra) Juniper—Often junipers are found in dry, rocky areas at higher elevations particularly in the Desolation Wilderness. Junipers over 1000 years old have been found in the Tahoe area. They have an appearance similar to incense cedars with reddish, brown bark. They rarely exceed 50 feet in height. Those growing in windy, exposed areas may be twisted and gnarled. The best way to tell the difference between juniper and incense cedar is that juniper has blueberry-like cones, and is usually found at higher elevations.

Wonderful Wildflowers

Wet Areas: Meadows, Stream Banks and Springs

Corn Lily—This poisonous plant looks somewhat like a stalk of corn, but smells like cabbage. Not only is the poison deadly, but it has been reported to turn its victims green. Corn lilies start out like a big cigar roll popping out of the moist meadows in the spring. By late summer it has grown to 3 to 6 feet tall. At the top of its broad-leaf stalk, it shows a large grouping of cream-white flowers.

Corn lilies

Cow Parsnip—A large wildflower with huge maple-shaped leaves, cow parsnip stalks can reach up to 10 feet tall but average 4 to 5 feet. It is often found in meadows, along creeks, or in other moist areas. It has several tall stalks with tight white button flowers that look like miniature cauliflower heads at the top.

Crimson Columbine—The most commonly seen columbine of the Tahoe area has numerous bright red-orange flowers that look like miniature Chinese lanterns hanging off tall thin stalks. It grows to about 3 feet high in moist meadow areas and along streambeds.

Delphinium or Larkspur—Towering larkspur or larkspur delphinium have tall narrow stalks with beautiful small purple flowers that bloom all along the stalks. They are found in large numbers in some meadow and stream areas and provide a dramatic display, especially when they reach their maximum height of 6 to 8 feet. *Nuttall's larkspur* is a smaller variety at only about 1 foot high; it is found in limited numbers in dry or wet areas.

Elephant Heads—Sprouting off the foot-tall green stalks are numerous tiny pink flowers that have little trunks and elephant-shaped ears. While not as showy as other meadow plants like columbine and tiger lilies, elephant heads are often seen in spring and early summer in Tahoe Meadows and especially in Meiss Meadows.

Monkeyflower—There are 11 species of this plant in the Tahoe area, all having flowers supposedly resembling little monkey faces. The most common are the pink Lewis' monkeyflower and the yellow common monkeyflower. They favor the banks of small streams or seeps throughout the Tahoe area.

Monkshood—This relatively uncommon plant is found in moist areas. Its large deep purple flower resembles a monk's cowl. A tall plant that can reach 6 feet, monkshood grows among the tremendous variety of flowers found near Marlette Lake as well as in the Page Meadows area.

Shooting Stars—Found in moist meadow areas, shooting stars have delicate petals that bend back to expose the darker stamens, thus making them like streaking night stars. The *alpine shooting star* has pink flowers, while the *Jeffrey's* has a purple-to-pink flower with a black point and a small band of yellow just above the black.

Tiger (Alpine) Lily—Often found with columbine in wet or marshy areas, the tiger lily can grow 4 to 6 feet tall and is a wonderful visual treat with bright orange flowers speckled with brown.

Tiger lily

Dry and Sunny Areas

Checkermallow—Along with mule ears, this is perhaps the commonest flower in dry, volcanic areas. It is found at lake level and up to over 9000 feet and is a low-lying flower with small pinkish-purple cups threaded by white veins.

Douglas or Sierra Wallflower—This bright-yellow flowered plant is common in dry areas and on rocky slopes. A member of the mustard family, it has a big cluster of little yellow petals forming a ball atop a straight green stem. It reaches a height of 1 to 3 feet.

Fireweed—Fireweed grows in profusion along old road cuts and areas that were

Fireweed

recently burned, disturbed, or where most of the plant cover has been removed. It seems to be most prolific after drier-than-normal winters. The plants are 3 to 4 feet high and covered with bright pink flowers.

Horsemint—Horsemint is found in abundance in dry meadows and rocky flats (Tahoe Meadows is one example). It is identifiable by its purple corn-cone group of flowers situated on top of a green stem with many green leaves. It is related to pennyroyal.

Mariposa lily

Mariposa Lily—The beautiful round white flowers of the Mariposa lily have a purple-to-black center and a delicate appearance. Three cream-white petals form a small bowl. This plant is usually less than 6 inches tall and prefers dry or sandy soil on sunny open slopes.

Mountain Pennyroyal or Coyote Mint—This common flower grows in open forests and along volcanic slopes. A member of the mint family, pennyroyal has white or pink flower clusters atop upright stalks. It provides a strong mint smell as you walk by.

Mule Ears—In areas with open, south-facing slopes, and particularly with volcanic soils, the mule ears are often the dominant flower species. They can cover acres of land with very few other plants in view. When you see a field of mule ears, you will also smell them as they have a strong odor. Big yellow sunflowers and large leaves that resemble the ears of a mule lend the plant its name. In the fall, the leaves dry up and turn brown, and make a rustling noise in the wind.

Prettyface—These relatively common flowers grow close to the ground and have 6 light yellow petals at the end of each flower stem. Each petal has a small dark purple line extending toward its tip. Large groups of "pretty faces" can be found looking at you from dry soil.

Scarlet Gilia—The bright red-orange beauty of scarlet gilia is startling to behold when it appears in the dry sandy forest and on open slopes. It can get up to 3-feet tall and has many bright trumpet-shaped flowers.

Deep Forest Pinedrops—The pinedrop is a saprophyte, which means that the plant obtains its nutrients from decaying vegetation in the ground rather than through photosynthesis. Pinedrops grow to 3-feet tall and have orange-red to reddish-brown stalks with numerous little curlicues coming off the sides of each narrow stalk. After they die they often remain standing for years, turning darker as years go by.

Snowplant—Snowplants are also saprophytes and do not require sunlight to grow; they appear from under trees or in dense forest areas. They are long and cylindrical (from 6 inches to 1 foot high) and a bright red color. Snowplant shoots straight out of the ground like a huge asparagus stalk, adding a splash of red color to the shade of the forest. They get their name because they pop up just after the snow melts.

Snowplant

Mixed Wet or Dry Areas

Asters and Daisies—There are several species of these sunflowers that have pale

Aster

purple petals circling a disk of yellow or gold. The *western aster* and *wandering daisy* are both quite common in the Tahoe area. Both plants grow up to 2 feet tall, although they are usually shorter, and occur up to 9000 feet. They prefer moist over dry settings.

Explorer's Gentian—This late-season bloomer has deep blue or purple tubular-shaped flowers. Light dots speckle the inside of the petals. Found in moist or rocky terrain, gentian provides a bit of bright color when many summertime flowers have come and gone.

Paintbrush—The orange *Red Applegate's paintbrush* and the *giant red paintbrush* are the two species most commonly seen in the Tahoe area. Both have flowers that look like the brush end of a bright orange and red paintbrush. Often they are called Indian paintbrush. These and other species can be found on dry slopes to wet meadows, up to 9000 feet.

Paintbrush

Shrubs and Bushes

Buckthorn, Snowbush or Mountain Whitethorn—This plant with many names grows along disturbed areas, along trails, and has lots of narrow white branches with spiny, thorn-like tips; when flattened by the snow, these branches lay down over the trail. I call it "mountain bikers' menace" because its thorns can puncture tires. Whitethorn is about 3 to 4 feet tall and spreads out over 5 to 10 feet. It has small ovate-shaped whitish/green leaves. Often the plants are so thick that it is difficult to determine where one plant ends and another begins.

Chinquapin—This common plant was named after a condominium project north of Tahoe City (or was it the other way around?).

Chinquapin is a bushy shrub related to oaks, that inhabits dry slopes and rocky ridges, and frequently grows near manzanita bushes. The narrow leaves of this 2 to 4 foot tall plant are up to 3 inches long, yellow-green on the top, and yellow-brown underneath. Chinquapin produces yellow-green, spring seedpods.

Huckleberry Oak—One of the most common plants in this area, huckleberry oak typically gets to about 3 feet high and grows on dry-south facing slopes. It has small leathery ovate leaves of medium to dark green. At the end of the narrow stalks you may see a light green acorn.

Manzanita—While there are five species of manzanita in the Sierra, only two are commonly seen in the Tahoe area. *Greenleaf manzanita* is widespread in dryer areas over a wide elevation range. Its smooth bark is dark red or reddish-brown with shiny, bright green leaves and it grows to about 3 to 5 feet tall. Manzanita has lots of rigid, crooked thick branches. In the spring they put out tiny pink flowers that supposedly look like little apples ("manzanita" is Spanish for little apple). *Pinemat manzanita*, with smaller leaves and stalks, is a smaller plant that grows to about a foot tall; it likes to form a carpet along the ground or over the top of granite rocks. Pinemat manzanita usually grows at a higher altitude than its greenleaf cousin. It is especially common between South Camp Peak and Kingsbury Grade.

Red Mountain Heather—This dwarfish bush has dark green conifer-like needles and clusters of small bright pink or red flowers on the top of short stalks. It grows at high elevations throughout the Tahoe area, along some lakeshores, and in the Desolation Wilderness. This fragile plant is a thick ground cover running alongside the trail so take care not to step on it.

Squaw Carpet or Mahala Mat—Thick patches as much as 10 to 20 feet across are made up of holly-like leaves carpeting the ground. In the spring, clusters of small blue-to-violet flowers grow among the sharp-edged leaves.

Thimbleberry—They may not keep you from starving in the woods, but thimbleberries are edible and quite tasty when they ripen in late August and September. They are in the same family as blackberries and raspberries and you will not be surprised to hear that the berries look like little thimbles. This bush is usually found in large groups lying close along the ground near streams and in other shady moist areas. Thimbleberry has large leaves that resemble a maple leaf with three to five pointed lobes. The showy white flowers bloom in early summer.

Tobacco Brush— This plant is also called snowbrush ceanothus and curlleaf ceanothus. Some say the strong pungent aroma of tobacco brush is sensuous and aromatic; to me, it smells like tobacco. With large, shiny, dark greenish-blue leaves, the plant grows up to 5 feet tall and has numerous small white flowers. Tobacco brush likes dry disturbed areas along road cuts and trails and can become the locally dominant plant.

Bikers heading toward Watson Lake. Note forest fire in the distance.

hikers and horses: in other words, horses have the right-of-way on the trail. In the mid-1990s an article appeared in the Tahoe Rim Trail *Newsletter* written by Sonja Willits, a woman with years of experience riding horses on Sierra trails. Willits did a good job of explaining trail use from the horse's point of view. With her permission, I've summarized the main points below.

- *A horse believes that everything will eat it until proven otherwise.* The first instinct of many horses is to run away, which can endanger both horse and rider, as well as anyone in the flight path who could get trampled or knocked off the trail. It is the job of all humans—equestrians, hikers, and mountain bikers—to assure the horse that no harm is intended.
- *When you are approaching a horse from behind, be sure to talk to the rider.* This lets the horse know that you are not something that will hurt it. A bike that comes speeding up from behind a horse can severely frighten it. Be particularly cautious when rounding blind corners—horse riders often can't hear you coming.

Half Moon Lake and Jacks Peak from south side of Dicks Pass

- *When you see a horse coming toward you on the trail, talk to the rider.* Again, this soothes the horse and assures it that you are not a threat.
- *When approaching a horse going down a hill, pull over to the downhill slope of the trail and allow the horse to pass.* Spooked horses often want to go uphill.
- *If you are in a group of more than one biker or hiker, encourage everyone to move to the same side of the trail when you encounter horses.* Horses can feel trapped between you if you are standing on either side of the trail. An entrapped horse is not a good thing.
- *Wait to change clothes, repack your backpack, or make any sudden moves until the horses have passed.* While you are stopped, waiting for a horse to go by, it may seem perfectly fine to take off a shirt or rearrange things. As far as the horse is concerned, your movement and changed appearance may add to its feelings of being threatened.

Most horseback riders will move off the trail when it is easy

✓ Tim's Quick Tips for How To Be an Inconsiderate Backcountry Blockhead

- ✓ Make a lot of noise.
- ✓ While people are relaxing and enjoying the quiet at a mountain lake, yell at your friends on the other side of the lake.
- ✓ Let your dogs bark; when they take a swim, let them shake off on people you don't know.
- ✓ While you are walking along on the trail, talk loudly so that everyone within a half mile can hear you.
- ✓ If you are camping, make lots of noise late at night and again early in the morning. When you are in the quiet woods, it's party time!
- ✓ Loud stereos especially appeal to your average nature lover.
- ✓ Camp or sit close to other people. When you encounter a solitary person at a beautiful mountain lake, they obviously need some companionship and nonstop chatter.
- ✓ Don't worry about your garbage; someone else will pick it up. Anyway, it should biodegrade in a couple thousand years.

Leave things in your campsite, so everyone knows you were there. It's a way to mark the good spots.

- ✓ Stay on the trail in people's way when they are trying to get by. If people are riding up a hill, stand in their way so they have to get off their bikes; they will enjoy the struggle to get back in their pedals on a steep hill.
- ✓ When you are walking or riding along the trail, ignore someone else wanting to pass. What's the hurry?
- ✓ Wash your dishes and clean your fish in streams and lakes. Fish thrive on detergent and consider bits of processed cheese to be great delicacies.
- ✓ Feed the animals. That way you help train them to get food from the next hiker who comes along. Backpackers get to practice the art of keeping animals out of their packs in the middle of the night. You can train some chipmunks and squirrels so well that they will practically jump into your lap to get a snack. While they can carry bubonic plague, the risk is a small price for well-trained squirrels.
- ✓ Leaving food out at night for bears is even more fun. The sound of a bear rampaging through your camp gives you a better rush than a double espresso.

Lake Aloha

for them to do so. They don't expect hikers and bike riders to give way all the time, particularly when the trail is especially narrow or precarious. However, it is the job of bike riders and hikers to step to the side first, and it is important to have some basic understanding of horse and rider psychology in order to be a conscientious sharer of the trail.

Hikers Take Note

In recent years, mountain bikers have taken great strides toward more environmentally and socially-sensitive use of the trails. It is also the responsibility of hikers to make an extra effort to get along with other trail users. If hikers use common sense and follow the basic rules of courtesy, everyone will benefit and more fully enjoy the trail. If hikers don't reciprocate, they may turn into the dreaded "Inconsiderate Backcountry Blockhead." Don't let this happen to you!

4 Weather, Water, and When to Go

Some basic knowledge about the weather and water availability in the Lake Tahoe area and along its Rim Trail will help you plan a safe and enjoyable trip. All outdoor recreational activities in the Sierra are greatly affected by weather conditions. Of particular relevance is how much precipitation, usually in the form of snow, occurred the previous winter. Sierra Nevada winters come in a wide variety of sizes and time frames. In some years, it begins to snow in October and doesn't stop until June. After a year like that, hiking on dry land is out of the question until the middle of July in most areas. The following winter may not see snow until late January, and then make up for it by dropping a lot of snow through May (a great year for late fall hiking). One season might have early heavy snow, followed by light snow, and then warm temperatures after February: this bodes well for those who want to get into the woods early to enjoy great wildflower displays and decent water availability.

Snowpack

The areas of highest elevation around Lake Tahoe often receive over 600 inches of snow annually. There are several factors for determining whether the place you want to go will be out of the snow in the spring or summer and some general rules governing the area's snowpack. Winter storms arrive primarily from the west, leaving lots of snow near the Sierra crest. There is less snow as you

Cross-country skiing near the Tahoe Rim Trail.

travel farther east from the mountaintops. The west side of Lake Tahoe gets considerably more snow than the east. (The east shore gets about 30 percent less snow on average at the same elevations as the west shore.)

Elevation—The amount of snow is greatly determined by elevation. As cold air lifts and passes over higher terrain, the likelihood and amount of precipitation increase. Storms progress across land forms and temperatures drop as you go up in elevation; the higher you go, the more likely it is that the precipitation will be snow. Over the course of a season, high elevations receive considerably more snow than lower elevations.

Which Way the Mountain Faces—Snow melts at different rates depending on which direction the mountain is facing and which side of the mountain you are on: north-facing slopes get less sun and stay cooler. Here, the snow melts more slowly. The difference between the snowpack on a north or south-facing slope can be quite surprising; it is not unusual to see 5 feet of snow on a north-facing slope, while on the south-facing slope the ground is bare and wildflowers are coming up.

Although the difference between north and south is more pronounced, east-facing slopes are also cooler and will have more snow than west-facing slopes. A classic example in the Tahoe area of the north–south difference is Emerald Bay. The Vikingsholm Trail and the trail along Emerald Bay to Emerald Point on the south-facing side of the bay are free of snow in most years at least one month before the trails on the north-facing side of the bay.

Lee of the Mountains: Away from the Wind and the Rain—The farther east you travel away from the western face of the mountains, the less likely for snow to fall. The mountains block and capture the snow and rain, leaving little moisture for the areas to the east. Consequently, the area around Serene Lakes on Donner Summit gets more snow than almost anywhere else in the United States, while just 40 miles to the east, and behind several mountains, Reno frequently receives less precipitation than any other major city in the United States.

The Wind, It Doth Blow—Winter winds create huge snowdrifts that resemble desert sand dunes. What does this mean to a hiker? There are areas where these winter dunes take longer to melt than other snow-packed areas, most commonly on the lee side of ridgetops where cornices form. These cornices can last well into the summer, while all around them wildflowers grow.

> **Trail Use Tip**
>
> Early in the season, your best bet for a hike or ride is close to the lake or in the Truckee area (lower elevations and in the lee of the mountains), on the east side of the lake (Carson Range), and at lower elevations. As the season progresses, different areas become available for snow-free travel, moving from east to west, and south-facing to north-facing.

Winter Wonderland

The winter landscape of the Sierra Nevada Mountains is both serene and pristine, with a beauty that you rarely find in the summer. In the winter, a soft white blanket covers the world with cold sparkles reflecting the blue sky. Walking or skiing through new fallen snow, you will find the rarest of gifts—peace and true quiet. In addition to the heavy snow fall in winter, you will also have some sunny winter days that provide wonderful opportunities to get out and enjoy all that deep white powder. Although many people prefer the winter as the time to enjoy the mountains and woods, this can be a more challenging and dangerous time. Unpredictable weather, unsigned trails, and other snow-related hazards are among the risk factors with which you should become familiar. Observe the weather and snow conditions. If the weather is getting bad, be smart, turn around and get out. Continually check your surroundings, observe familiar peaks, creeks, and other landmarks that will allow you to get back to your starting point if you are in a blizzard. Some of the most powerful blizzards can quickly become life-threatening. If you learn about mountain winter conditions and take a few simple precautions, much of the trail and areas in the Lake Tahoe area are great for winter snowshoeing or cross-country skiing.

Land without Visible Trails—The fact that the Tahoe Rim Trail is not signed for winter creates challenges for even the most experienced. Many popular winter spots may have tracks from the people who were there before you, but there are no real trails. You must follow landforms and head for saddles, mountaintops, or flats. Often, you may be heading in a general direction instead of to an exact spot. Know where you are and where you have been, and don't hesitate to follow your own tracks back out to where you began. It becomes even more important to have a map and follow it. Learn how to use a compass.

Dehydration—This is another serious risk when you are hiking, snowshoeing, snowboarding or cross-country skiing. With all that snow around, you still need to drink plenty of water. When the weather is colder, people tend to drink less even though they may actually need as much water as on a hot day. While you are at it, eat. You'll need the energy.

Hypothermia and Frostbite—When the body's core temperature is seriously reduced as a result of exposure to cold and moisture, hypothermia can result. This is a serious condition, aggravated by cold wind and sudden climate changes. The symptoms of hypothermia include shivering, loss of coordination and the ability to do simple tasks, and disorientation and confusion. The treatment is based on common sense: first, get the victim out of the wind and elements. Prevent heat loss by getting the victim into warm, dry clothes (you should be carrying extra clothing in your pack). Get the victim into a sleeping bag, if you have one, and climb in to add your body heat (although, be careful as this may lower your own body temperature). Give the victim warm liquids and high carbohydrate foods.

Frostbite is the freezing of body tissues due to prolonged exposure to cold. The most susceptible areas to frostbite are the feet, hands, ears and face. Prevention is the key for both hypothermia and frostbite. Remember a few simple rules: eat high-energy foods and drink plenty of liquids. Keep rested. Wear the right clothing and bring along layers. Don't do something that will get you wet, and get out of the woods if you

> ❄ **Tim's Quick Tips: Avoiding Winter Weather Risks**
>
> ❋ Keep an eye on the weather forecasts until right before you leave. Many great weather sources exist, including local radio and television stations (KCRA-Sacramento, and KOLO-Reno are two of them); The Weather Channel (on cable television); and, these websites —www.weather.com and www.writeonrex.com—are also useful.
>
> ❋ Before setting out, let someone know where you are going and when you plan to return.
>
> ❋ Bring extra layers of clothing. The weather may change for the worse even if the forecast is for nice weather.
>
> ❋ Do not venture out unless you know how to navigate without a visible trail.
>
> ❋ Use a compass and map.
>
> ❋ Bring your survival kit!
>
> ❋ Drink lots of water.
>
> ❋ Avoid situations that cause hypothermia and frostbite.

do get wet on a cold and windy day. Have an extra set of clothes in case you get wet.

Avalanches—Understanding how avalanches occur and how to avoid them is too big a topic for this book, but a few words of warning can help you avoid a tragedy. Remember that you are most vulnerable to avalanche when you are on moderately steep slopes (very steep slopes may not hold enough snow to avalanche), the lee side of mountains, or in gullies. Unstable snow conditions most often occur during or right after a storm; the bigger the storm, the bigger the risk. Obtain an updated avalanche danger report by going to www.avalanche.org or www. sierraavalanchecenter.org If you plan to do a lot of backcountry travel, I highly recommend taking a Level One Avalanche Course, which will teach you how to determine avalanche risk, and how to work with beacons and probes to rescue those who have been caught in an avalanche. For more information go to www.avalanche.org or www.sierraavalanchecenter.org.

Sunburn!—The bright sun makes the snow even more beautiful and white. At the end of the day you have beautiful memories, and one heck of a case of sunburn. Snow reflects the sun's rays like water and can burn your skin quickly. Use sunscreen and wear sunglasses to protect your eyes.

Guided Winter Hikes—The Tahoe Rim Trail Association runs a program of guided snowshoe hikes during the winter months. Past trips have included full moon jaunts in Tahoe Meadows and daytime hikes into Page Meadows. For more information go to www.tohoerimtrail.org.

Packing and Dressing for Winter Weather

Aside from sunblock, be sure to carry a basic survival kit! Your kit should include the following items:

The great ski race

☐ Two large plastic garbage bags (to be used as a poncho or emergency shelter in bad weather)
☐ Waterproof matches
☐ A plastic whistle (three short blasts means help)
☐ Candle
☐ Metal cup for melting snow
☐ Duct tape (for repairs, can be wrapped around the top of a ski pole)
☐ Cocoa or other powdered mix
☐ Cell phone (don't count on using it, however)

You have three goals when it comes to clothing yourself for outdoor winter adventures: keep dry, keep warm, and keep cool. To accomplish these goals, wear or pack clothing made of synthetic fibers. They are lightweight and whisk moisture away from your body which will help to keep you warm. Bring several lightweight layers of clothes, including a waterproof outer shell; it will help you stay dry but will allow you to remain cool if the temperature turns warm. Wear a sturdy pair of waterproof boots with two pairs of socks, a thin inner layer of socks made of synthetic fiber and a thicker outer layer of wool or synthetic fiber. Wear water-resistant pants, such as those designed for cross-country skiing; over these, wear a waterproof shell if you are snowshoeing or traveling through deep snow. A hat is essential, whether it is a baseball cap on a warm day or a warm fleece hat on a cold day. And, don't forget gloves: the style depends on the conditions and activity you are doing. If it is warm and you are doing strenuous cross-country skiing, lightweight ski gloves are fine. If you are out hiking or snowshoeing on a cold snowy day, bring a thicker, warmer pair of gloves.

When (and Where) To Go

Winter to Spring

For those who love the snow and winter sports, there are a number of places that are especially attractive and challenging for winter activities. Here are a few of the best spots:

Page Meadows—The easiest way to access Page Meadows in winter is through the Talmont Estates subdivision. From Tahoe City, go 2 miles south on Highway 89 to Pine Avenue. Turn right, then right again on Tahoe Park Heights. Go to the top of the hill where you will take Big Pine, the middle of three road choices. Follow Big Pine to Silvertip and turn left. There is limited parking available at the end of Silvertip. From the end of the road, head west a few hundred yards to the first of several meadows. The area around Page Meadows is especially popular for cross-country skiing and snowshoeing. The terrain is mostly level, perfect for beginners. The meadows are beautiful on a sunny day or at night when the moon is full.

Tahoe Meadows—Located on the south side of Highway 431, the meadow is great for a beginner on either skis or snowshoes. From Incline Village, drive 7 miles up Highway 431, the Mt. Rose Highway. Here, you will see a large treeless area on your

Hikers cool their feet in Lake Aloha.

right. Park along the road. Both the large open meadow and its surrounding forest are popular for winter sports; in fact, on a weekend you might find this area too crowded. Head south up through the trees to a saddle for extraordinary lake views. You could well be dazzled by lodgepole and whitebark pines covered with hoarfrost.

On the north side of the highway at Tahoe Meadows, the TRT climbs toward the radio tower and Mt. Rose, another excellent area to ski or snowshoe. While this route can get quite steep and difficult near the top, the views of Mt. Rose and Lake Tahoe from the radio tower are inspiring.

Spooner Lake Cross-Country Ski Area—Located at Spooner Lake near the intersection of Highways 50 and 28, this well-managed cross-country ski area provides access to Marlette Lake, Snow Valley Peak, and the Hobart Road area via over 90 km of beautifully groomed trails, some of which crisscross the Tahoe Rim Trail. Views of Lake Tahoe and the beautiful Snow Valley

Lake Tahoe from Tahoe Cross-Country Ski Area

are seen from the trails. At Spooner Lake Cross-Country, you can rent charming rustic log huts during winter or summer. For more information, contact them at (775) 749-5349.

Tahoe Cross-Country Ski Area—Located on Dollar Hill about 2 miles east of Tahoe City along Highway 28, Tahoe Cross Country is the venue for The Great Ski Race from Tahoe City to Truckee (which crosses the Tahoe Rim Trail). This wonderful area provides 65 km of trails through the forests between Mount Watson and Tahoe City. Many of this Nordic center's trails are popular with mountain bikers and hikers in the summer. Contact Tahoe Cross Country at (530) 583-5475.

Kirkwood Cross-Country Ski Area—Kirkwood is located 30 miles south of South Lake Tahoe on Highway 88. It has a network of over 50 miles of trails with spectacular views of the Carson Pass–Kirkwood area. For more information, call (209) 258-7248.

For additional information on winter trail use, take a look at *Snowshoe Trails of Tahoe* by Mike White, published by Wilderness Press. The Tahoe Nordic Search and Rescue Team has all kinds of valuable information and they are the guys and gals you will be really happy to see if you get lost in the snow. Some of the information in this section comes from the Tahoe Nordic Search and Rescue team's winter awareness brochure, "A guide to winter preparedness and survival." To obtain a copy, or for more information call (530) 581-4038. Above all else, if you have a phone, in an emergency call 911.

Summer to Fall

Summer and early fall at Tahoe are mostly sunny, warm, and glorious. Nevertheless, afternoon thunderstorms do come up. During some summers there may be no thunderstorms while in other years, they may occur almost daily. Usually storms are scattered, developing—sometimes out of a clear blue sky—during mid-to-late afternoons when the temperatures are warm and a great deal of tropical moisture has moved in from the south. Keep your eye on the large and high darkening clouds moving rather quickly in your general direction. Better yet, check out the weather information channel or local weather broadcasts and plan accordingly. You can also log on to www.theweatherchannel.com or www.writeonrex.com.

The chance of a thunderstorm need not thwart or curtail your plans, but do bring your rain gear. Sometimes the storm moves swiftly through a specific area and drops only a little rain before it passes. However, if the storm gets exciting and lightning starts to flash, get out as quickly as possible, especially if you are on an exposed peak, near bodies of water, or under tall trees. Avoid areas of high exposure, such as the top of a pass. Dicks Pass, for example, is not a good place to be in a thunderstorm. Avoid the urge to take shelter under a solitary tree in open lands. If you cannot get out of the woods in time, it is best to stay in the forest in an area of similar-sized trees. While lightning can be scary and dangerous, it is also important to remember that it is rare that someone is actually struck by a lightning bolt. Absent a bit of very bad luck, if you take reasonable precautions you should be fine.

Water

Much of the Tahoe Rim Trail is located along ridgetops, a perfect situation for enjoying the sublime views of Lake Tahoe and the surrounding mountains. However, its rim-top location results in a shortage of water along many sections of the trail, especially on the sections along the east shore. Plan ahead and make sure you have enough water to get you through the section you will be hiking. On hot summer days, you will need at least 2 to 3 quarts of water. Water is an especially important issue to consider if you are planning on thru-hiking the entire TRT.

Be sure to avoid drinking any untreated water in the Sierra Nevada. Giardia, a microorganism that occurs in many bodies of water here, can create havoc in your intestines. To prevent giardia or other bugs from getting into your system, be sure to filter, boil, or treat with iodine any water that you draw from a natural source.

In each section of the trail described in chapter 6, additional specific water information is provided.

5 Fun for All and All for Fun: A User's Guide to the Tahoe Rim Trail

During spring, summer, and fall, many types of users enjoy the Tahoe Rim Trail, each with particular needs, all with the same general goal of having fun, enjoying nature, and challenging themselves on the trail. Because one user's mode of transport on the trail—whether it is a pair of legs, a pair of wheels, or four strong horse hooves—can impact another's, this chapter will focus on the different types of users and offer tips and suggestions for a mutually safe and pleasant journey.

A Hiking Paradise

Most people who buy this book probably enjoy hiking already and know the basics: carry plenty of water, wear comfortable boots or shoes, take a map, guidebook and sunscreen, and bring extra clothes in case of a change in the weather. Chapter 6 has complete descriptions of each section of the Tahoe Rim Trail, plus information about short spur trails that hikers can add to customize their outings. Every section of the trail offers something unique, whether it is the scenery or the specific challenge of the route.

To get the most out of your journey, take care of a few simple things before you leave. Most importantly, tell someone where you are going, when you expect to be back, and check in when you return. Although the Tahoe Rim Trail is not as isolated as a lot of backcountry areas, you may still be alone on many parts of it. It

Hikers near Relay Peak

is only common sense to leave information with a friend or family member as to your general whereabouts. Much of the Tahoe Rim Trail is primarily used by daytime users, so late in the day you are most likely to be alone on the trail. In the following sidebar, you'll find a checklist of key things to remember when you are planning your Tahoe Rim Trail trek.

Backpacking and Camping

Why not hike the whole Tahoe Rim Trail? Depending on how strong a hiker you are, it takes anywhere from 10 days to 3 weeks to totally encircle Lake Tahoe on this route. (Such a hike is called a "thru-hike.") Two weeks would be a comfortable period (although two weeks of backpacking and comfort are not usually seen in the same sentence). The TRT is a loop trail so you could start anywhere and end right back where you began.

A backpacking trip of this length requires some logistical planning. Your primary concerns will be where to camp and where to get water and additional food. Camping is allowed everywhere on the Tahoe Rim Trail except in Desolation Wilderness where you must obtain a permit in order to camp. For more information, call (530) 573-2674. Although permits are not required in Lake Tahoe Nevada State Park, camping is limited here to two primitive campgrounds, each with a pit toilet and picnic tables. For more information, call (775) 831-0494.

To find out where else you can camp, refer to the trail descriptions in Chapter 6. For water availability, review the "Heads Up" section at the beginning of each trail description. If you are hiking in late summer or fall, keep in mind that some of the water spots may have dried up. If you come to a major water source in the fall, be sure to fill up, but be sure to boil, filter, or treat the water before drinking it.

The good news (or bad depending on your perspective) is that

✾ Tim's Top Tips For Backcountry Hikers

✾ Bring more water than you think you will need.

✾ Don't drink the water in lakes and streams unless you boil, filter, or treat it.

✾ Carry a first-aid kit. If you take something out, don't forget to restock.

✾ Dress in layers. Don't wear cotton except on hot dry days in midsummer.

✾ Wear good hiking boots or a comfortable athletic shoe. Some hikers prefer the newer high-quality hiking sandals.

✾ Wear a liner sock and a heavier outer sock (find what works for you; I often now hike with one hiking sock)

✾ Bring enough clothes; temperatures can change quickly.

✾ Carry and use sunscreen.

✾ Bring rain gear—the weather can change rapidly in the Sierra.

✾ Start out early when it is still cool and there are fewer people on the trail.

✾ Bring a map and this guidebook. A good field guide is also useful to have along.

✾ Tell someone where you're going and when you expect to return; check in when you return.

✾ If your knees hurt when you hike, try using hiking poles; these can make a significant difference when you hike downhill and help to balance you when you are needing to scramble over a rocky section of trail.

✾ If you have recently come from a much lower altitude, take time to acclimate yourself to a higher altitude before you set off.

Hikers in Desolation Wilderness

a lot of people live at Lake Tahoe who have built communities with stores that carry every amenity you could possibly need.

Road Crossings and Drop-Off Points

Your backpacking trip can be designed so that you can pick up food and supplies at various locations and trailheads along the way. In between the stops, where you may have arranged to meet friends, you will need water. Here is a summary of the road crossings and communities that you will encounter along the TRT.

Tahoe City (Sections 1 and 8)—The trail route goes right through Tahoe City, a good midway stop-off point if you started your trip at Echo Summit or Kingsbury Grade. As you cross the road from one section of the trail to the next, you will be within 100 yards of a supermarket, and within half a mile of several motels; these are often booked-up in the summer so call ahead and warn them to have the showers ready. Tahoe City is loaded with outfitters who will be happy to sell you any equipment you may have forgotten or need to replace. Check out Alpenglow located near the trail on North Lake Blvd., the main road that goes through the center of town.

Kings Beach (Sections 1 and 2)—The trail crosses Highway 267 at 2.75 miles northwest of Kings Beach. A supermarket is located near the intersection of Highway 267 and Highway 28, with most of the supplies you may need. This road crossing is a good place for a friend to drop off food or water, or you could leave a stash of water here in advance. Very little water is available on the section of trail between Tahoe City and Brockway Summit; when you cross Highway 267, the next water source is a spring beyond Mud Lake or Gray Lake, both over 10 miles away. The spring may run dry by fall, so don't count on it for your only supply.

Incline Village (Sections 2 and 3)—The TRT crosses Highway 431 at 8 miles above Incline Village. This is another place to meet your wonderful friends who have brought you fresh supplies. Be sure to load up on water at Ophir Creek, about a mile along the trail after you cross Highway 431. If you are heading south during a dry year, the next water source directly on the TRT may be over 35 miles away.

Spooner Summit/Highway 50 (Sections 3 and 4)—There are no towns nearby, but this first road crossing in 23 miles may be a good place to stop and get replenished by those now great friends of yours (your "trail angels").

Daggett Pass (Sections 4 and 5)—At the top of Kingsbury Grade, you will have the joy of walking several miles to the next trailhead through a subdivision and the Heavenly Ski Resort. Ah, but they have food and drink and lodging available, and you walk right by the Tramway Market. Perhaps they would even be willing to hold a box for you, so call (775) 588-8666. This may make a good spot for a major stop or planned meeting place. In addition,

Stateline and South Lake Tahoe are only 4 miles away down the Kingsbury Grade.

Highway 89, Big Meadow Trailhead (Sections 5 and 6)—You have just hiked 23 grueling miles and you get to the road where there is nothing except a bathroom. Use it. This is another good drop-off point where your loyal friends can bring you food acquired in nearby South Lake Tahoe or Meyers. If your friends don't show up, or you are in an emergency, Meyers is about 5.3 miles downhill from the trailhead.

Echo Summit/Resort (Sections 6 and 7)—After 17.5 more miles past Big Meadow Trailhead, you reach the Echo Lakes Chalet (530) 659-7207 which has a store. Stock up because Barker Pass Road is 33 miles north. On that road it is an additional 11 miles to the next store. The Echo Chalet has a seasonal post office open during the summer months where you can pick up a package of food that you were smart enough to mail to yourself before you left on your excursion. Or, you can mail food to the next town post office, Tahoe City, 49 miles away. Echo Chalet sells excellent sandwiches and ice cream, both highlights when I arrived there on Day 11 of a TRT thru-hike.

Barker Pass (Sections 7 and 8)—This remote road crossing is located over 11 miles from Tahoe City via Barker Pass Road and Highway 89, and could work in a pinch as a drop-off point.

Ward Creek Road (Section 8)—The trail crosses this road halfway between Barker Pass and Tahoe City. If necessary, you could have asked someone to meet you at this road crossing to supply moral support and give you the news of the day, but Tahoe City is only 5 more miles away.

While depending upon your friends to assist with your thru-hiking plans is certainly desirable, if that doesn't work out you may have to make arrangements yourself. This means caching wa-

Big Meadow

ter ahead of time in a few of the driest sections—placing a gallon or two near the trailhead a few days before your departure. It also means either mailing food packages to yourself or picking up food along the way. Tahoe City, with great outdoor stores and several supermarkets just a short distance off the trail, is your best bet for resupplying on the trail.

What To Bring in Your Backpack

My good friend and hiking buddy Shannon Raborn hiked the entire 2100 miles of the Appalachian Trail that runs between Georgia and Maine. When she told me what to bring on a spring/summer/fall backpacking trip in the Sierra, I listened. I thank Shannon for her helpful contributions to the following list, which we wrote together.

First, you will want to organize your pack by the object's use. Remember, the less weight and space taken up, the better off you will be as you carry it down (and up and down again) the trail:

Clothes—Hiking shorts, shirts (made of lightweight, preferably light synthetic fibers), warm fleece shirt, rain shell, several pairs of socks, Tevas, Crocs, or water socks (for around camp), baseball

Tahoe Rim Trail Association

hat, warm pants or convertible pants that are shorts during the day and pants at night. If it is very cold, fleece hat and gloves.

Toiletries—Toothbrush, toothpaste, vitamins, and medications, sunscreen, toilet paper, biodegradable all-purpose soap, and scrubby sponge for cleaning pots, pans and your hands. Pack any scented product in a scent-proof container and remember to store it in a bear canister when you sleep at night.

Camping Supplies—First-aid kit, tent, rope, Thermarest pad, sleeping bag (lightweight is best), backpacking pillow (a luxury, but it feels SOOOO good!), camp stove (I like Jet Boil's all-in-one pot and stove, with gas canisters), gas for stove, water filter and/or iodine tablets, water bottles, Camelback (optional but very nice, especially because it enables you to carry large amounts of water, necessary on the dryer sections of the TRT), trowel (pooper scooper), lighter and/or matches, pot/pan kit, bowl, cup, utensils (spoon, fork, knife), knife, compass, headlamp or flashlight, map, heavyweight garbage bags (to keep things dry in case of rain), duct tape, field guides, this book of course, and camera.

If you are "camping light," and the weather forecast does not include rain, and it is past mosquito season (late summer), you could forego the tent and tent fly. If you do not mind going without cooked food, you can also eliminate the stove, stove fuel, and pots and pans. Keeping your clothes to a minimum is another technique to lower weight, but be sure to not cut out something you may need.

Bear Canisters—In areas with lots of bears (anywhere near Lake Tahoe), bear canisters are essential. Canisters not only work well at keeping out small animals such as squirrels and marmots, but they can serve as a chair or as a wash tub for doing your laundry.

Food—Plan what you need, but keep it light. Remember that John Muir only took some biscuits with him! Freeze-dried dinners are tasty but they can be expensive for a long trip. I especially like the ones that you can just add hot water. Some recommended food items are: instant oatmeal, pasta, couscous, soup, energy bars, gorp/trail mix, bagels, salami, hard cheese, avocado, tortillas with stuffing such as cheese or cooked chicken, crackers, hot chocolate or coffee, fruit packages, cereal, powdered milk, cookies, and tea.

Yippee! Mountain Biking

When the Tahoe Rim Trail was first built, mountain biking was not allowed anywhere on the trail. As time went by and regulations eased, the trail become about 50 percent open to mountain

Tim's Top Tips for Mountain Bikers

Ride only where bicycles are permitted.

Wear your helmet.

Speed is your friend: hitting the brakes too hard or going too slowly over a rocky section can send you flying over the bars. With a little speed you can bounce right over the rocks (of course, if you fall, the rule has now changed to "speed is your friend, until it isn't.")

To prevent undue erosion, avoid wet, muddy areas.

Spring and fall temperatures, which would be bearable when you're hiking, get bone-chilling as you cruise downhill at 20 miles an hour. When it's cold, try a warm ski hat under your helmet, warm socks, and lots of layers. Your legs will be pumping so they won't get as cold, but the wind goes right to your neck and through those bike shoes.

Wear bike shoes, bike shorts, and bike shirts; they are well designed to make your ride more enjoyable.

Wear a Camelback or other water-hydration system: mountain biking is strenuous exercise and a water bottle just isn't sufficient on a warm day. Additionally, a Camelback lets you drink without stopping and keeps the water colder throughout the whole ride.

When riding downhill, lift your bottom slightly off the seat, lean back gently, don't grip the handlebars too tightly, and flow down that awesome single track. (Don't forget to yippee!)

Learn how to fix a flat and do minor repairs on your bike; bring a spare inner tube.

Scrapes and cuts are common while biking, carry a small, light First Aid kit in your pack. One good brand is the Optimist by Adventure Medical Kits.

Happy biker near Tahoe Meadows

bikers. It is important to understand that the Tahoe Rim Trail is really only suitable for intermediate and advanced riders. Most sections are quite difficult and technical, so riders should make sure they are capable of riding the section before setting out.

The areas closed to bikers include the approximate 50 miles of the route that overlap with the Pacific Crest Trail. Bikes are also forbidden in the wilderness areas: Desolation Wilderness and Mt. Rose Wilderness. Also, a section of trail going north from Spooner Summit past Snow Valley Peak to Hobart Road does not allow bikes. Bikes are permitted on the rest of the TRT.

For detailed descriptions of each section of the trail, directions on how to get to trailheads, and special sidebars applying to bikers, refer to individual trail descriptions. A summary of which sections you can or cannot ride on is provided below (these are also shown on the maps).

Section 1: Tahoe City to Brockway—Riding is allowed on the entire section.

Section 2: Brockway to Mt. Rose—Mountain biking is allowed between Brockway Summit and the Mt. Rose Wilderness Boundary, a distance of about 7 miles. If you start from the Tahoe Meadows end there are two trails, one which allows mountain bikes and one which does not. Follow the instructions for that section. Either way you can go only 4 miles to the Relay Peak Tower on your bike.

Section 3: Tahoe Meadows to Spooner Summit—Mountain biking is allowed between Tahoe Meadows and Hobart Road, which is 14.3 miles (for the section between Tahoe Meadows and Tunnel Creek Road, which is 9.2 miles, mountain biking is allowed only on "Even" days of the month). At Hobart Road, a detour is available down to Marlette Lake and then out to Spooner Lake via North Canyon Road.

Section 4: Spooner Summit to Kingsbury Grade—This entire section is open to bikes.

Section 5: Kingsbury Grade to Big Meadow—This entire section is open to bikes, but much of it is very difficult.

Section 6: Big Meadow to the Pacific Crest Trail—Bikes are allowed from the Big Meadow Trailhead for about five miles to where the Tahoe Rim Trail meets the Pacific Crest Trail in Meiss Meadows. Bikes are not allowed on the Pacific Crest Trail.

Section 7: Echo Summit to Barker Pass—Bikes are not allowed on this entire section, which overlaps with the PCT.

Section 8: Barker Pass to Tahoe City—The first 5 miles are on the PCT; bikes are prohibited on the PCT. From Twin Peaks to Tahoe City, bikes are allowed.

Getting Horsey on the TRT

For most horseback riders, the entire Tahoe Rim Trail is a great place to ride. While some equestrians may find a few sections difficult (Desolation Wilderness and an area south of Barker Pass especially), almost all of it is very good for riding. Water is a concern on much of the trail, especially on the east shore. If you are planning on riding the TRT, be sure to read through trail descriptions for detailed information. While on the trail, watch out for other users. Horses are supposed to be given the right of way, but be alert and cautious just the same. Horses are fairly rare on the TRT so other users may not expect to see them. Many experts suggest equestrians always wear helmets. Learn the trail ahead of time, and be sure to maintain a comfortable pace for yourself and your horse. Stay on the trail to protect the fragile environment. There are two other issues that equestrians must consider before embarking on a ride along the TRT.

Where To Park the Trailer

Tahoe City—There are two parking locations close to the trailheads. Both can be crowded with narrow access. The first is at the "64 Acres" (Truckee River Access) parking lot located on Highway 89, 0.25 mile south of its intersection with Highway 28 in Tahoe City. From here, you can ride along a paved road for a short distance and then meet the TRT heading toward Page Meadows.

The second Tahoe City parking spot is located at the Fairway Community Center on Fairway Drive, directly across the street from the Tahoe Rim Trail section which goes from Tahoe City to Watson Lake, and then on to Brockway Summit. From the Tahoe City "Y" (the intersection of Highways 89 and 28) go 0.2 mile on Highway 89 toward Truckee and turn right on Fairway Drive. Drive 0.2 mile to the Fairway Community Center on the right. If you park at the "64 Acres" and ride toward Watson Lake, it can be challenging because you must cross a busy bike bridge here, walk

Horses at Dardanelles Lake

on a congested section of bike trail, and then cross Highway 89 to walk 0.2 mile on Fairway Drive.

Brockway Summit—There are two parking areas available here. You can park along the road at the TRT parking area, 0.5 mile east of Brockway Summit, which only has room for a few cars and would require you to unload your horse near a busy road. The second location is 0.2 mile past the top of Brockway Summit toward Truckee. On the right is a road leading up to Martis Peak. This is a great spot for horses and from here you can ride your horse up the lightly traveled Martis Peak Road several miles until you meet the TRT.

Mt. Rose/Tahoe Meadows—The Tahoe Meadows Trailhead parking lot was designed for horses, but may be congested on a busy day. If no spaces are available, a shoulder is available on the meadow side of the road. After you park, follow the sign toward Brockway Summit or Spooner Summit. If heading toward Brockway Summit from this trailhead, use extreme caution, as you will have to ride parallel to, and then cross, the very busy road to the trailhead. There is also limited parking at the Mt. Rose Trailhead.

Spooner Summit—Both trailheads on Spooner Summit have convenient places to park your trailer. It is best to park on the side of the road where you will begin your ride so you do not have to cross Highway 50, a major highway with cars roaring by at high speed.

Kingsbury Grade, North—The north trailhead of Kingsbury Grade has room to park your trailer along this quiet subdivision road.

Kingsbury Grade, South—The large Heavenly Ski Area Stagecoach parking lot should provide plenty of room to park your horse trailer.

Big Meadow—The Big Meadow Parking lot has parking spots designed for horse trailers, but the access is quite narrow. Often the horse-parking spots have been taken by cars in this crowded parking area (if you do not have a horse, give those with horses a break and park in the other spaces if they are available). The parking lot has some winding, sharp turns that can be a challenge. If you are heading toward Freel Peak, you can park along the road near the Grass Lake trailhead and then use this connector trail.

Echo Summit—At the top of the summit on the south side of the road is a large snow park that makes for a great spot to park your trailer. From here, you can ride across the parking lot and head south, or follow the trail north to Lower Echo Lake. There is also parking at Lower Echo Lake, although this can be full to overflowing on summer weekends.

Barker Pass—There is plenty of parking space available at the top of Barker Pass. From here, you can head in either direction on the

Tahoe Rim Trail. The paved road up to Barker Pass is a good one, but has a few narrow, twisting turns.

Places to Horse Camp

When looking for a place to camp when you are backpacking, the primary considerations are finding water and a pretty spot. When you have a horse, another concern enters the picture: where do you find grass for your horses without destroying a beautiful meadow? Equestrians should bring their own horse feed instead of relying on unpredictable and fragile grass and meadowlands.

Some of the good camping spots for horses include:

- **Watson Lake**
- **Ophir Creek**—Go straight at the TRT/Ophir Creek Trail junction to a nice spot near the creek, but out of Tahoe Meadows. You are now on Ophir Creek Trail, but close to the TRT.
- **Star Lake**
- **Armstrong Pass**—Take the Armstrong Pass connector trail down to the dirt road and a nearby stream. The dry meadow area is known as Horse Meadow.
- **Meiss Meadows and the area near Showers Lake**
- **Desolation Wilderness**—See permit information in Chapter 4.
- **Ward Canyon, below Twin Peaks**
- **Robie Equestrian Park**—This special 160-acre wilderness equestrian park serves as the staging area for the annual Tevis Cup 100-mile horse ride from Tahoe to Auburn. While not on the Tahoe Rim Trail, the equestrian park is located 3 miles from Watson Lake, and has two trails with direct access to the TRT. Accessible by vehicle, it is a convenient place for horse camping or setting out for day rides. Livestock water, outhouse facilities, and ample

Lower Echo Lake

parking are available. The park is open to day-use through-out the summer. Reservations for overnight camping are needed in advance. Contact the Wendell and Inez Robie Foundation at P.O. Box 714, Foresthill, CA 95631, phone (530) 367-4332, or email: robiepk@foothill.net.

Goin' Fishin'

Rainbow trout, brook trout, brown trout, and cutthroat trout are the most common fish in the mountain lakes and streams around Lake Tahoe. In a few lakes, including Lake Tahoe itself, you will also find kokanee salmon and Mackinaw trout (which has edged out the cutthroat in the lake). Most mountain lakes are stocked with fish on a regular basis, although there has been talk of ending the stocking program, especially in wilderness areas. This could greatly affect the mountain fishing experience.

Fishing on the Rim Trail is just like anywhere else: a fishing license is required for anyone over 16 years of age. To obtain a license, contact your local sporting goods store. If you have questions about fishing regulations in California call the California

Department of Fish and Game at (916) 358-2900. In Nevada, call the Nevada Division of Wildlife at (775) 688-1500.

Much of the Tahoe Rim Trail lies along the ridgelines surrounding the Lake Tahoe Basin. It is generally above the lake areas and the major streams that support fish populations. However, there are several locations along the trail that are good for fishing, and a number of spur trails to take you to good fishing sites. In general, since most of the lakes and streams are above the west shore, that is where the best fishing opportunities are.

Since half the fun of fishing is discovering your own secret hole, I am only going to reveal the more popular places below.

Desolation Wilderness/Western Rim—The area between Echo Lakes and Barker Pass has an abundance of fishable lakes. Explore the area and you will find the best spots to fish.

Truckee River—In Tahoe City the TRT meets the Truckee River, a popular fishing spot. During summer months this area is also popular with rafters. It is best to fish in early morning or late afternoon, or you may catch a big raft instead of a trout.

North Shore—Watson Lake, which is a fairly shallow lake, is pretty much your only choice in this area. Two other lakes in the area, Gray Lake and Mud Lake, do not have fish and are sometimes not even lakes.

East Shore—Only a few lakes of any size exist on the east shore. Close to the trail and right off the highway is Spooner Lake, a catch-and-release fishing area only. Marlette Lake is also catch and release. Because the shallow Twin Lakes often dry up in late season, they lack fish, but Star Lake, at the base of Jobs Sister, has trout.

South Shore/Meiss Meadows Areas—In this area, the Upper Truckee River, Meiss Lake, Dardanelles Lake, Round Lake, and

Showers Lake provide opportunities for fishing. In recent years Tahoe's native fish, the Lahontan cutthroat, has been reintroduced to these waters.

The best way to make sure that Tahoe area waterways continue to have fish is to practice the catch-and-release fishing technique. Create barbless hooks by smashing the barb on your hook with a pair of pliers. Once you catch the fish, treat them gently. Remove the hook while the fish is still in the water and release it back into the environment where it belongs. If you are camping and really would enjoy a fish dinner, go ahead, but be sure to only take the fish you will eat (and don't clean the fish in the nearest lake or stream).

For more details about fishing in the Sierra, refer to *Sierra Trout Guide* by Ralph Cutter, published by Amato Publications. It provides a list of every lake in the Sierra and what kind of fish may be found there. Or check out Ralph's website at www.flyline.com. Another informative source is the *Desolation Wilderness Fishing Guide* by Jerome Yesavage, also published by Amato.

Kids Like to Hike . . . Some Kids. . . Sometimes . . . and, Not Too Far

The Tahoe Rim Trail is a challenging trail for grown-ups because it traverses terrain that has lots of elevation gain. Much of the trail is simply not suitable for younger children. There are, however, a few great destinations for family outings. Here are a few suggestions on my favorite places to take children. The complete route descriptions are in Chapter 6.

Mt. Rose/Tahoe Meadows Area—Near the top of the Mt. Rose Highway at Tahoe Meadows, the Tahoe Rim Trail has two trailheads and an interpretive trail. All three provide an opportunity for kids to learn about and enjoy the mountains. Each of these trailheads is located above 8000 feet, about 7.5 miles up Highway

Kids love the Echo Lakes water taxi.

431 from the intersection of Highway 28 and Highway 431 in Incline Village. They are all in the same vicinity or across the street from each other.

Tahoe Meadows Interpretative Trail—If you are coming from Incline Village, on Highway 431, you will see a parking area and a building set down below the road on the right hand side after about 7.5 miles. This marks a trail, which has been built to be wheelchair and stroller accessible, a very easy 1.3-mile loop. The trail starts on the eastern edge of the lower parking area and winds through the meadow. It is a great spot for early summer wildflowers and a place where the little ones can stretch their legs. This is the easiest segment of the Tahoe Rim Trail and would be suitable for very young children.

Tahoe Meadows to Spooner Summit—This hike starts from the western edge of the same parking lot as described just above. First, the trail traverses Tahoe Meadows and passes a display of

Take them before they grow up!

wildflowers, a few small streams, and the larger Ophir Creek—a playground for kids. Once you have crossed the meadow, the trail levels out and heads uphill, not too steeply, to the top of a saddle located at 1.7 miles from the trailhead. From the saddle, the trail levels off again and remains mostly level for several miles with only a few gentle up and down passages. The views of the lake are incredible and there are numerous flat rock "armchairs" inviting you to enjoy your lunch or a snack. Walk as far as you want and then turn around. This area is also a great spot for someone who is learning how to snowshoe or ski cross-country.

Tahoe Meadows/Mt. Rose to Brockway Summit—From Incline Village, on Highway 431, drive past the main Tahoe Meadows trailhead on your right and go another 0.7 mile, where you reach the Mt. Rose/TRT trailhead with restrooms and parking. For your family outing, hike up the trail.. Lake Tahoe, Tahoe Meadows, and the mountains around the lake quickly come into view. In 2.5 miles of fairly easy walking you reach lovely Galena Falls and then shortly cross two streams and find great mid-season wildflower displays. At the junction with the Mt. Rose trail you can turn around for a 5 mile out and back, or turn left and follow the trail up to a dirt road, which will lead you on a 5.7 mile loop.

Big Meadow Area—Drive 5.3 miles south of Meyers on Highway 89 to the Tahoe Rim Trail Big Meadow Trailhead. This trail heads northeast toward Kingsbury Grade, or south 5 miles to where the Tahoe Rim Trail intersects the Pacific Crest Trail. If your children are hearty, they may enjoy the hike south where, after about 3 miles and approximately 800 feet of elevation gain, you will reach Round Lake. Along the way, you will traverse through lovely Big Meadow. You will also encounter some huge volcanic rock formations. The lake itself is a great respite for the kids. (You could also take the spur trail to Dardanelles Lake, a beautiful lake located 3.4 miles from the trailhead).

Echo Lakes Area—At Lower Echo Lake (see directions in Chapter 6, Section 7), you will find a store, a small marina, and a large parking facility. From the lake, your trail is the Tahoe Rim Trail, Tahoe-Yosemite Trail, and the Pacific Crest Trail all combined; it heads north. The first 2.5 miles go along the Lower and Upper Echo Lakes and provide great views of the lakes. This trail has some fun up-and-down passages and rocky scrambles, perfect for any 10 year old.

At the end of 2.5 miles, you can continue on the trail, turn around, or take the Echo Lakes Water Taxi back to the Echo Lakes parking lot. The taxi is a small boat that crosses back and forth across the lakes. It only operates seasonally, so be sure to check ahead for taxi times and to make sure it is running. The taxi pier is a great place for a swim while you are waiting for the boat. Late in the summer the lake level drops too low to allow passage for the taxi between Lower and Upper Echo Lakes. For more information about the Echo Lakes Water Taxi, contact Echo Chalet at (530) 659-7207.

Another option is to take the taxi to the end of the two lakes and cut out 2.5 miles of a trip to Lake of the Woods or Lake Aloha. If you take the water taxi, it is only about 3 miles to Lake of the Woods, and 3.5 miles to the eastern edge of Lake Aloha. I found Lake Aloha to be a perfect spot to take my child on a back-packing trip. Be prepared for a hearty climb of about 1000 feet through rocky terrain.

Page Meadows Area—The Page Meadows area can be approached from several different directions and is an excellent and easy place to take the kids on a hike. Probably the easiest way into the area is through the back of the Talmont Estates/Twin Peaks subdivision. Take Highway 89 south about 2 miles from Tahoe City. Turn right on Pine Avenue. In about 0.2 mile, turn right on Tahoe Park Heights. Follow Tahoe Park Heights to the top of the hill and then take Big Pine, the middle of three roads. Continue on Big Pine for about 0.25 mile to Silvertip Drive where you turn left. Follow Silvertip to the end of the road and park where you see a sign that reads SKI PARKING. A dirt road heads west from the end of the road. Follow it down the hill straight ahead until you pass a sharp left-hand turn. Just after the turn, a single-track trail heads off to the right and arrives at the first meadow in about 100 yards. Follow along the edge of the meadow until you see a trail heading left (west) through the meadow. From here you can start exploring. The trail goes by several big meadows. The meadows provide tremendous mountain views, great wildflowers in the summer, and lots of aspen trees making it prime for fall colors. Bring a picnic lunch and a Frisbee and have at it with the kids. Avoid trampling in the fragile meadow area, at least until late summer or fall when the area has had a chance to dry out.

Ward Canyon Area—On Highway 89, drive 2.4 miles south of Tahoe City, past Sunnyside Resort to Pineland Drive on the right. In 0.4 mile this becomes Twin Peaks Drive. Stay on the left at the Y and in about 0.1 mile the road becomes Ward Creek Boulevard. Take this about 1.5 miles to a TAHOE RIM TRAIL sign on

Dogs love Round Lake.

your left where the trail begins. Follow the old road as it parallels the largely unseen Ward Creek for the next 3 miles. Go as far as you want and then turn around. The trail eventually leads rather steeply up to Twin Peaks, but that would be a long haul for the little ones. The first 3 miles, however, are just a gentle uphill with lots of wildflowers in season, Ward Creek nearby, and wonderful views of the Sierra crest above.

For more information about hiking and backpacking with children, pick up a copy of my book *Monsters in the Woods: Backpacking with Children*, published by University of Nevada Press.

What About Fido?

While dogs are allowed on much of the Tahoe Rim Trail, restrictions do apply at several state parks, including Lake Tahoe Nevada State Park. In fact, regulations governing dogs on trails completely depend on what county you are passing through. It is your responsibility to know what the specific regulations are under each county's jurisdiction. In general, it is best to leave the pups at home or, at least, keep them on a leash. Dogs off leash chase and interfere with wildlife, and trample the understory of forests. Your chances of encountering wild creatures will increase and you'll have the satisfaction of knowing that you are limiting your impact on the trail. If you do hike with your pooch, be sure to have him or her on a leash or under voice command at all times. Dogs jumping on other hikers, chasing mountain bikers, running beyond your sight line, or harassing horses are a big no-no. If you have a well trained, on-leash animal that doesn't go after every squirrel or chase every lizard, by all means take him or her along.

6
Trail Descriptions

Throughout these trail descriptions, mileages are given from point-to-point. Mileage figures were based on several sources; the primary sources for the maps you see in this book are Tom Harrison's "Lake Tahoe Recreation Map," which has been enhanced with information generously provided by Jeffrey P. Schaffer, whose *Tahoe Sierra* and *Pacific Crest Trail: Northern California* set the standard for guidebooks in this area. These figures will give you distances between certain locations. However, you should realize that when it says 0.9 mile, another source might report it as 1.1 mile. If this difference really bothers you, perhaps you need to relax a bit. I have found the best way to relax is to spend time walking in the woods. For your convenience, a mileage chart for the Tahoe Rim Trail appears in Appendix A.

Before each description, I recommend when the section can be hiked without encountering large amounts of snow. These dates are estimates based on an "average snow year," but in reality there is no such thing as an average year. It either snows more than average or less than average. The dates should give you a rough idea of when you can hike. If it has been an especially mild winter and a warm spring, you could expect to hike the trail sooner than the dates stated here. Refer to Chapter 4 on weather for more detail on snow seasons.

Finally, the Tahoe Rim Trail is constantly evolving. Minor trail changes for maintenance and realignment are being planned and implemented on a regular basis. Although this book attempts to be up-to-date, changes to the trail may have been made since this book was published. For more information on any recent changes to the trail, contact the Tahoe Rim Trail Association at (775) 298-0012.

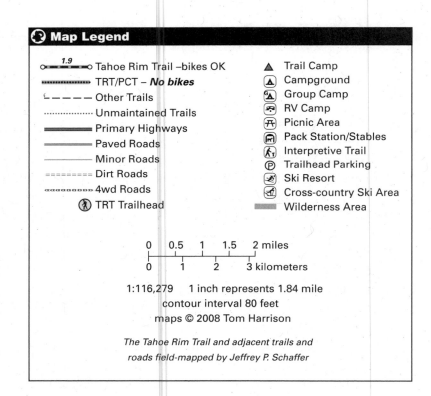

Tahoe City to Brockway Summit

(19.2 miles)

Difficulty—This section is strenuous. It is long and requires a good deal of climbing, and can be quite hot in the summer when it is also mostly waterless. During the first 3 miles, sharp rocks on the trail might be hard on the feet.

Best Seasons—While portions of the trail at lower elevations can be utilized from late May to early November, higher elevation areas keep the snow until later. The snow melts first along the first several miles north of Tahoe City.

Highlights—This section includes a pleasant open forest with a wide variety of plants. Much of the area has been extensively logged over the years, so you will see mostly smaller, newer growth trees. Views of the lake are found in several locations. You can also enjoy mountain views of Twin Peaks, Alpine Meadows, and Squaw Valley from several places along the trail. Watson Lake, while not the most beautiful lake along the Tahoe Rim Trail, is a pleasant shallow lake nestled among the trees you will find two-thirds of the way through your hike.

Heads Up!—This is a long stretch and water is in short supply. No year-round water sources exist except for Watson Lake located 12.5 miles from Tahoe City and 6.7 miles from Brockway Summit. Watson Lake is shallow and has water that does not look enticing to drink. (These days, you should treat water from even the most sparkling lakes.) A stream east of Watson Lake may be available in the early season. Bring lots of water if you're hiking this section! With many road crossings and much off-highway-vehicle (OHV) use, don't be surprised to hear or see cars close to the trail. Watson Lake can be accessed via a paved road and is heavily

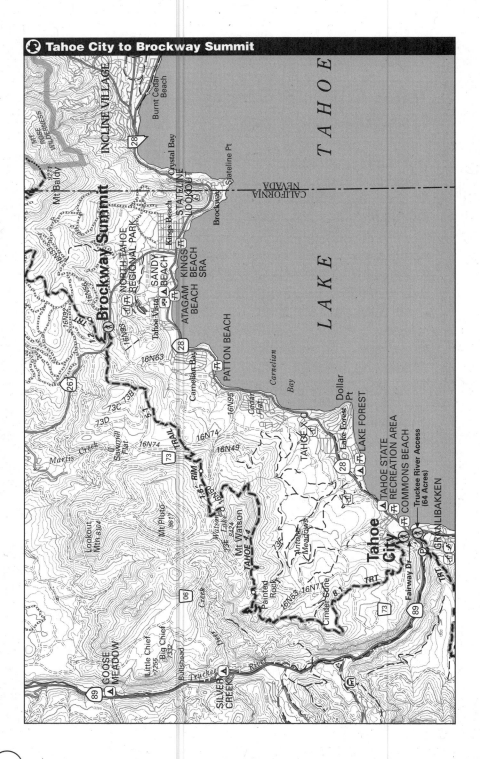

Pacific Crest from Tahoe Rim Trail north of Tahoe City

used by car campers and occasionally by late-night partiers. For mountain bikers, the rocky terrain can be challenging, even frustrating. This section is not recommended for beginner riders.

Getting There, Tahoe City to Brockway—From the Tahoe City "Y" at the intersection of Highways 89 and 28, go 0.2 mile west on Highway 89 toward Truckee. Just past a gas station (a Chevron at the time this book is published), turn right on Fairway Drive. Drive another 0.2 mile to a parking lot and the Fairway Community Center on the right. If this parking lot is full, you can park (weekends only) at the Tahoe City Public Utility District offices about 0.1 mile back toward Highway 89. Your trailhead is across the street from the center.

Getting There, Brockway to Tahoe City—From the intersection of Highway 28 and Highway 267 in Kings Beach, drive 2.75 miles north on Highway 267 to the TRT trailhead. Look carefully—it is easy to miss. Parking is available at the road pullout on the left, at 0.5 mile before Brockway Summit. The trail starts right at the downhill edge of the parking area. If you plan on mountain biking this section, it is best to head south from Brockway Summit toward Tahoe City, although either direction will challenge you with steep, rocky terrain that includes technically challenging sections.

Note: The Tahoe Rim Trail Association and Forest Service plan to reroute the first few miles of the Tahoe City to Brockway section. The aim is to take it out of the more rocky terrain and reduce the grade. Check with the TRTA for the status of the realignment.

Trail Description

From the Tahoe City trailhead, the trail starts out as a moderate 10% uphill grade and passes through thick sections of manzanita and patches of squaw carpet, and through a forest of white fir, Jeffrey pine, sugar pine, and incense-cedar trees. After about 0.7 mile you cross a dirt road; for a little history lesson, detour right and climb steeply uphill about 100 yards and then turn right. You will see a white cross that sits above Tahoe City. (See sidetrip "Boyles Last Ride.")

Back on the Tahoe Rim Trail several lake views open up through the trees as you head steadily uphill over very rocky terrain. You are traversing through a fairly thick, mixed forest of Jeffrey pine, white fir, and incense-cedar. About 2.25 miles in from the trailhead you see an expansive view to the west of the Twin Peaks ridgeline and Squaw Valley. The climb has become easier and the trail more rocky, with fewer trees

SIDETRIP Boyle's Last Ride

According to local legend, William Boyle was an easy-going codger with a dry sense of humor who lived in Tahoe City in the early 20th century. He once asked his drinking buddies to bury him above the town so he could keep an eye on them. True to their word, his friends dragged Boyle up the hill on a sled and buried him above Tahoe City on February 4, 1912. Shortly afterward, the cross was erected at the site. Photos taken at that time period show a clear, treeless view down to the lake. Now, however, trees and brush have grown so thickly that much of the view from the cross has been obscured.

on the meager soil. About 0.3 mile past the view, you make the first of many crossings of a major dirt road that locals call the Fiberboard Freeway (alias Road 16N73, Forest Route 73), after the company that once was the principal landholder in the area. The term "freeway" is derived from the fact that this wide gravel road is the main backcountry route linking Tahoe City and Brockway Summit (and via another connection, Truckee). After crossing the road, continue gently uphill over rocky terrain for another 0.5 mile to a viewpoint on top of some lava rocks, about 3.4 miles from the trailhead. Walk carefully over boulders to the high point, which lies clearly about 100 yards east, to see stunning views of Lake Tahoe to the southeast, and Mt. Watson to the northeast.

The trail now turns west and ascends gently across the rocky terrain and sparse forest, until at about 4.1 miles from the trailhead you pass the dark-red volcanic rock known as the Cinder Cone on the right. Longtime Tahoe locals will tell you that this cinder-cone area was the repository for Tahoe City sewer water before the treatment plant was built in Truckee in the 1970s. Does that change your mind about where you planned to stop for lunch? As the trail skirts the Cinder Cone you will see the remnants of an old fence. (See sidetrip "Cinder Cone.")

As you continue on the trail, which curves southwest, you will pass the Cinder Cone and soon reach the east rim of the Truckee River canyon. From here you get stunning views west into Alpine Meadows valley, as well as southwest to Ward Canyon in the distance to the left. Finally, after the long meander west around the cone, the trail heads north for 0.5 mile and then descends rather steeply (those who crossed the

> **SIDETRIP Cinder Cone**
>
> If you would like to see the Cinder Cone itself and avoid a bit of walking, leave the trail and walk northwest beyond the fencing. You'll be on the mostly flat, red surface of the Cinder Cone. The lack of plant growth and evidence of filled-in ditches clearly show that the site was once impacted by human use. Continue northwest toward the ridge. In less than 0.25 mile you will intersect the Tahoe Rim Trail.

Lava boulders near Watson Lake

Cinder Cone rejoin the trail before this downhill). A small north-facing section in thick forest here may hold a remaining patch of the previous winter's snow. Soon, you reach an open saddle at the end of a little-used dirt road, 5.0 miles from the trailhead, and then begin heading gently uphill through an open forest of fir trees and manzanita. Quickly the trail proceeds downhill and the forest becomes thicker and your hike shadier.

Like most of the northern and western shores of Lake Tahoe, this area has been heavily logged in the past. The most extensive logging occurred in the late 1800s when much of the Tahoe Basin was logged to make braces in the silver mines of nearby Virginia City to keep them from collapsing (as well as for lumber and fuel). Loggers at that time focused on the best trees for their purposes—the pine trees, especially the majestic sugar pine—and left most of the fir trees. During an extended wet period, the red and white firs took over the territory from the more drought- and disease-resistant Jeffrey and sugar pines, creating an unnaturally dense forest of firs primarily. If nature had been allowed to revert to its own natural process, periodic forest fires would have thinned the population of fir. Instead, the federal and state governments, under heavy pressure to prevent forest fires and to limit tree cutting, had a policy of preventing major forest fires by putting out all fires as quickly as possible. In the short-term this policy saved the forest, but it led to a denser forest, and increased the likelihood of a catastrophic fire. We now know that this historic policy excluded the ecological role of frequent natural fires. Adding to the danger, in the early 1990s when annual precipitation was below normal for several years in a row, many trees died when they were unable to resist the debilitating impact of the bark beetle. Expansive stands of dead trees in an overly thick forest are a recipe for disaster. The National Forest Service and both the Nevada and California State Park Departments began an aggressive effort of salvage logging and controlled burning to reduce the danger. As you walk or ride on the Tahoe Rim Trail, you may see evidence of this effort in many locations in the form of brush piles waiting to be burned and stumps from recent logging.

About 1 mile past the last dirt road, you cross another dirt road. (See sidetrip "The Wall.") This one is in a dry gully above the headwaters of Burton Creek. Those desperate for water can head 0.75 mile southeast down the road to its end at the Fiberboard Freeway (Forest Route 73). Turn left there and head briefly north to the creek. (This may dry up after a mild winter.)

To continue on the TRT, you will cross this second dirt road to enter prime mountain-biking terrain. The amount of trail traffic will increase dramatically. The trail here is part of a network of trails providing great biking opportunities out of Tahoe City and the Tahoe Cross-Country Ski Area located in the Highlands subdivision. The next stage is a mostly

> **SIDETRIP "The Wall"**
>
> A left turn here would quickly take you 300 yards northwest to a minor saddle and the start of a steep downhill, known as "The Wall" by mountain-biking enthusiasts. It leads to the Western States Trail and in a few steep downhill miles to the bike trail at the bridge across the Truckee River between Squaw Valley and Alpine Meadows. The bike trail leads back to Tahoe City and the beginning of the TRT; this makes a nice loop for bikers.

moderate climb through soft volcanic dirt and mixed forest 0.9 mile to the east edge of Painted Rock (7754 feet). Along the way you'll pass some impressive volcanic boulders. After the climb to Painted Rock, you're rewarded with two good viewpoints: one offers a panorama southeast toward Lake Tahoe; another spot a little farther on gives you an awe-inspiring view into Squaw Valley backed by the Sierra crest.

After all the uphill work you have done in the last 7 miles, you get a break with a mostly shady descent (or if on a bike, a really fun downhill) to another crossing of the Fiberboard Freeway at about 8 miles from the Tahoe City trailhead. Here, usually on the first Sunday in March, The Great Ski Race passes this point on its way to Truckee. This 30-kilometer cross-country ski race, from the Tahoe Cross Country Ski Area on Dollar Hill to Truckee, attracts up to a thousand people, making it one of the biggest cross-country ski events in the western United States. For the next 0.8 mile you cover a smooth, gentle incline over hard-packed sandy soils (mountain bikers should ride it back down to know one of the best biking stretches on the whole TRT). Where the trail levels off and runs into an old narrow dirt road, a left turn will take you 100 yards north to the Fiberboard Freeway. (See sidetrip "Mt. Watson.")

Just south of the Fiberboard Freeway, take the TRT; it turns right and follows an old abandoned dirt road, now overgrown with manzanita and tobacco brush. This gentle downhill stretch continues 1.6 miles, providing several excellent lake views before a left turn heads you back uphill. You now wind uphill, northeast, between lava boulders

SIDETRIP **Mt. Watson**

A left turn at the Fiberboard Freeway will take you back to Tahoe City, while a right turn will take you to Truckee, Brockway Summit, or to the top of Mt. Watson. Should you want to climb or ride to Mt. Watson, follow the Freeway uphill from where it meets the dirt road for 0.7 mile to a junction with a major dirt road that turns sharply right (southeast). Turn onto this road and follow it for 1 mile on a 640-foot ascent to the top of Mt. Watson (8424 feet). Views from the top are glorious; you can see most of Lake Tahoe and its surrounding mountains as well as Squaw Valley and Alpine Meadows to the west.

and cliffs for the next 0.75 mile to a wonderful stopping place among several especially large boulders, with enticing views of the lake to the south between the boulders. That large white-roofed building in the foreground is my alma mater, North Tahoe High School. Beyond the viewpoint, the trail levels off and turns right before it reaches another junction, 1 mile short of Watson Lake. (A left turn here would take you steeply uphill to the top of Mt. Watson.)

Continue straight ahead on the TRT on a moderately steep downhill toward Watson Lake. Just before the lake, you reach a gravel road; turn left on this road and follow it uphill. In a short distance, the TRT takes off to the right and skirts the east shore of Watson Lake. While little Watson Lake is pleasant enough, it is shallow, surrounded by trees, and visited by numerous mosquitoes. It can also be heavily used in the summer since it is the only lake between Brockway Summit and Tahoe City, and accessible by car along a paved and gravel road. At all times be sure to filter water at Watson Lake if you think you may need more water before the end of the route.

After you pass the lake, with 12.5 miles under your belt and 6.7 miles to go, the TRT heads about 0.25 mile north to a shallow gully. The trail now descends gently 1.25 miles east through beautiful wildflower meadows and forested areas, to a road, down which you can head 0.3 mile to usually reliable Watson Creek. You pass several small seep streams that provide water until midsummer. Since these are the last water sources along this section, take advantage of the opportunity if it's still available. Just 0.25 mile east beyond the road, a short (90 yards) spur trail leads off to the right to a large rock pile with another pretty view of Lake Tahoe, specifically Carnelian Bay. Enjoy the view—it's the last full lake view you'll get before reaching the Brockway Summit trailhead in about 4.5 miles.

The trail turns north and in 0.8 mile switchbacks down through a thick forest of white fir and Jeffrey pine to a crossing of Forest Route 74, and 100 yards farther crosses Forest Route 75.

After a gentle descent northeast for about two-thirds of a mile, you cross another road, then traverse about 200 yards to yet another. Now you have a fairly gentle climb for 1 mile as the trail takes you through manzanita and chinquapin before it crosses Forest Service Road 73 (Fiberboard Freeway). There is still more climbing for 1.3 mile until you cross the Fiberboard Freeway one more time. The next 0.7 mile gently descends to the trailhead, located next to Highway 267. At this point, you are about 0.5 mile east of Brockway Summit.

SECTION 2

Brockway Summit to Mt. Rose Summit

(19.7 miles)

Difficulty—With much of this section of the trail rising above 9,000 feet and some of it over 10,000 feet in elevation, it is relatively strenuous, especially considering you start at around 7000 feet. If you are day-hiking this section, it might be easier to begin from the Tahoe Meadows side and hike to Brockway Summit, where your starting elevation would be approximately 8800 feet. As they say, 1800 feet here and 1800 feet there and eventually you are talking about some real elevation gain.

Best Seasons—The entire trail can be hiked between late July and mid-October. The first 5 miles from the Brockway end can be hiked as early as June, but most of the trail is not free of snow until mid-July. The highest sections of the trail are among the first places to be covered with snow in the fall.

Highlights—The middle part of this trail section is mostly exposed, south-facing volcanic slopes with sandy soils. This wide expanse at a high altitude features tremendous panoramic views of the lake and a wonderful feeling of remoteness. Two small lakes are found on the trail, or close to it: small Mud Lake and Gray Lake, a prettier, knee-deep lake that is 0.5 mile off the Rim Trail via an access trail. A lovely waterfall, several streams, and a prolific wildflower display await you in the last 3 miles of your route.

Heads Up!—Since much of this hike is at high altitude, the air is quite thin, which can cause problems for those unaccustomed to high altitudes. If you feel faint, it may be due to reduced oxygen levels rather than the beauty of the views. Much of the trail is exposed to cold and wind, or to the hot sun. The first 5 miles can be tedious, but the remainder is a wonderful high-altitude

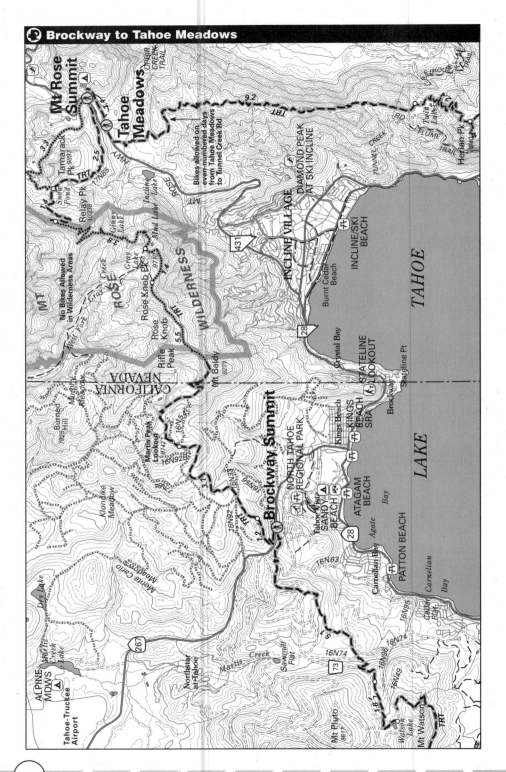

Bikes allowed on even-numbered days from Tahoe Meadows to Tunnel Creek Rd

No Bikes Allowed in Wilderness Areas

Above Tahoe Meadows

experience. Though water can be collected from several seasonal streams, and from Gray Lake and usually from Mud Lake, the supply is severely limited. A small seasonal spring exists about 50 feet below where the TRT meets the old Western States Trail (now abandoned) after Mud Lake. Gray Lake is about 0.5 mile downhill from a saddle just past Mud Lake, and Mud Lake itself lives up to its name by becoming a mud puddle by late summer. About 2.5 miles from the end of the trail, you'll find a small pond (known as both Snow Pond and Frog Pond) across from the trail to Mt. Rose. About a mile farther, water can be found cascading down from Galena Falls and crossing under the trail.

Tips for Mountain Bikers—If you are looking for a good section of the Tahoe Rim Trail to ride, this is probably not the one to choose. Please do not ride in the portion of this trail that does not allow bikes! The soil is quite fragile and easily damaged.

From the Brockway Summit side, bikes are allowed for the first 7.6 miles. It begins with a steady, technical, and sometimes steep climb of 4.3 miles to a major gravel road. From here you can take a left turn and head back to the highway on the road. On the way back to the highway, you will pass Martis Peak Rd., which will take you up to the Martis Peak Fire Lookout, with spectacular views to the north. Back on the TRT you could turn right and ride another mile, but it gets even steeper and more technical and may not be worth the effort.

The TRT from the Mt. Rose Summit trailhead to Snow Pond has two alternate routes. The first parallels Highway 431, 0.5 mile to a dirt road, where you turn right and ride 2.1 miles to the Pond. This route allows mountain bikers and horses. The second route, which begins to the right and above the bike route, allows only hikers. From the Snow Pond it is a steep and rocky uphill for 1.5 miles on dirt road to the radio tower, which is the end of the trail for bikers.

Getting There, Brockway to Mt. Rose Summit Trailhead (Tahoe Meadows) From the intersection of Highway 28 and Highway 267 in Kings Beach, drive 2.75 miles northwest up Highway 267 toward Brockway Summit to the Tahoe Rim Trail trailhead. At this point, you will see a parking pullout on the left and a steep dirt road on the right (Forest Service Road 16N56). Park on either side but this trailhead is on the right, or uphill side. If you reach Brockway Summit at the top of the hill you have gone 0.5 mile too far.

Getting There (Mt. Rose Summit Trailhead to Brockway). Take Highway 431 (Mt. Rose Highway) to Tahoe Meadows, then on to the trailhead just at the summit of the Mt. Rose Highway. The Mt. Rose trailhead is 8 miles from the Intersection of Highway 431 and Highway 28 in Incline Village, and 0.7 mile from the Tahoe Meadows South trailhead. It is directly across the highway from the Mt. Rose Campground, which can be a great camping spot for thru-hikers or as a way station the night before beginning your TRT hike.

Alternative Routes: The Tahoe Rim Trail Association will eventually take the trail off the road between Relay Peak and the Snow Pond. Instead, a trail starting near Galena Falls will switch-

Tamarack Peak

back up to the ridge, and then on to Relay Peak. In addition a trail to be known as the Rim to Reno Trail will connect the outskirts of Reno with the Mt. Rose Trail and the Mt. Rose Trailhead. As always, check the TRTA website, tahoerimtrail.org, for the latest information.

Trail Description

From the Brockway trailhead, cross the busy road carefully if you are parked on the south side of Highway 267, and follow the dirt road uphill (east) 100 yards to the trail and trailhead sign. The trail leads off to the left into the trees. This first section is no-nonsense, fairly steep, with occasional views of the lake as you switchback through a thick forest of newer growth Jeffrey pines and white firs. Walk quickly to escape the drone of automobile traffic from the road below. After about 0.5 mile, the views get better as you pass through an area of manzanita and squaw carpet. In early summer you will also encounter numerous wildflowers. Listen closely you may hear the mating call of a blue grouse. (Sounds like a bass drum, "*brmmmmm, brmmmmm, brmmmmm.*")

SIDETRIP View from a Rock

On your left is a short spur trail, which heads 0.3 mile up to a pile of rocks that look as though they were part of a set for "The Flintstones." From atop the rocks, you get great lake views to the south, and mountain views to the north and west. This is a very popular summertime spot to catch the last rays of the sun, and if you are camping, a good spot to see the sunrise.

After about 1 mile of steady climbing, you reach a junction at 1.2 miles from the trailhead. (See sidetrip "View from a Rock.")

The TRT continues straight ahead on a ridge, descending briefly before leveling off. Here it becomes more open; you will see fewer trees in a more scattered pattern, along with mule ears, a very common plant with large leaves and large yellow flowers. About 0.7 mile past the spur trail, you cross a gravel road (16N33) about 150 yards east of its junction with the paved Martis Peak Road. You start heading up again gently, before another short downhill to a small grassy opening with early summer flowers and a streamlet providing water in the springtime.

Next, head steeply up again through a forest that is transitioning from Jeffrey pines and white firs to the higher-altitude lodgepole pines and red firs. The air is thick with the pungent cinnamon aroma of tobacco brush. Your climb eases and you come out of the forest into a huge field of equally aromatic mule ears. Continuing uphill you leave the thick forest and the scenery changes dramatically. You reach an open rock pile, almost 4 miles from the trailhead that hosts dramatic views to the south of Lake Tahoe. Looking to the south across the lake, you can see (clockwise from east to west) Snow Valley Peak (9914 feet), the highest peak above the east shore; Jobs Sister (10,823 feet); Freel Peak (10,881 feet); South Lake Tahoe; Mt. Tallac (9735 feet); Desolation Wilderness and the Crystal Range; Twin Peaks (8878 feet) above the west shore; and finally Squaw Valley and Northstar. Freel Peak and Jobs Sister are the two highest peaks in the Tahoe Basin. If you continue on the TRT for another 64 miles you will walk just below Freel Peak as you cross a saddle at 9730 feet. If you enjoy sitting in the sunshine while eating your lunch, this south-facing spot may be just the ticket. On September 22, 2001, this viewpoint was the location for the official opening dedication ceremony for the Tahoe Rim Trail.

When you can drag yourself away from the panoramic views of the lake, continue up rocky terrain along the edge of a ridge. You will have a clear view of Mt. Baldy to the east, and the beautiful aspen groves along its flanks. With Mt. Baldy as your goal, you pass a rocky viewpoint to your right, and a field full of mule ears to your left, before heading back into the woods again briefly before reaching a major dirt road at 4.3 miles in from your trailhead. (See sidetrip "Martis Peak Lookout.")

This dirt road makes a good alternative trailhead for those who would like to hike 15, instead of 19, miles. At 8400 feet elevation you can also eliminate 1400 feet of climbing by beginning here. To access the dirt road, turn on Martis Peak Road, which is about 0.5 mile north of Brockway Summit. Follow this paved road as it climbs up and up and at a big left turn 4 miles in, the dirt road heads straight ahead. Go about 0.2 mile to the trailhead on your right.

> ### SIDETRIP Martis Peak Lookout
>
> A left turn on this dirt road will take you to the Martis Peak (8742 feet) lookout. To get there go 0.2 mile and then turn right and take the paved road 0.7 mile up to the lookout at 8656 feet. From here you will see excellent views of most of Lake Tahoe and the crest that rims it to the south, and to the north, most of the lands from the Donner Pass and Lake environs east into western Nevada.

The TRT turns to the right and follows the dusty road about 0.25 mile north to a fork. Keep left and gently ascend 300 yards north to a trailhead with parking for several vehicles. You have now reached a part of the old Western States Trail, also known as the Capital-to-Capital Trail because it once linked Carson City (the capital of Nevada) with Sacramento (the capital of California). The trail starts east through forest and alternating open rocky sections and in 0.5 mile reaches a saddle with views north. The tree composition is transitioning again with more red firs and occasional junipers, western white pines, and the first hemlocks that

Rockpile near the California-Nevada border above Lake Tahoe

you will see on this section. Your climb becomes steeper as you switchback 0.3 mile up to a ridgeline that has views into a large U-shaped valley, the drainage area for Juniper Creek, which empties into the Truckee River. After about a 300-yard traverse southeast on the ridgeline, the trail angles south for a 0.4-mile traverse of gentle slopes to a road; from here, the trail ascends 0.2 mile south to the road's end and the resumption of trail tread. In less than 0.5 mile you climb first moderately southeast, then moderately northeast up to the ridgeline. There's a great view here, but even more superlative ones lie ahead. Just 0.2 mile south you reach a low rock pile immediately west of the trail. This has dramatic views of the lake to the south, and mountains to the west and east. In addition, there are great views to the north in which you can see Castle Peak, Donner Lake, the town of Truckee, and Boca and Stampede Reservoirs.

From this view, you are now about 6.8 miles from the Brockway Summit trailhead. The TRT goes briefly east to the ridgeline, where you cross into Nevada. (This is a good place to turn around if you are on a bike.) As the trees get smaller and fewer, and you get higher, now above 9000 feet, the ridgeline area

Looking southwest toward Dollar Point and Pacific Coast.

opens up. Only the hardiest trees, such as lodgepole pine, western white pine and whitebark pine grow here. On the north-facing slopes below, and also east of you, snow may last well into the summer. After climbing moderately southeast 0.5 mile up the ridgeline, the TRT angles northeast, traversing just under a minor summit on a high ridge, which is 9271-foot Mt. Baldy. Just past it, you enter the Mt. Rose Wilderness. At about 7.6 miles from the trailhead, this is the end of the section of trail permissible to mountain bikes. Bike riding is not allowed in the wilderness. (A better place to turn around would have been the viewpoint you just passed, or where the trail met the dirt road, at 4.3 miles from the Brockway trailhead.)

Now you traverse the side of an open southeast-facing slope with incredible expansive views to the south and east of Lake Tahoe, Incline Village and beyond. For the next 2 miles, with the exception of a brief uphill foray into the forest, you walk beneath a volcanic ridge eastward on a gentle ascent over wonderful light brown sandy soil through huge open fields of mule ears. Views of the lake are truly glorious with almost the entire lake displayed before you. It is a real highlight of the Tahoe Rim Trail, and considering how far you are from either the Tahoe Meadows or Brockway trailheads, you may even have it all to yourself.

About midway on your northeast traverse you pass just beneath a steep-sided 9499-foot summit, behind which lies unseen, flat-topped Rifle Peak. In 0.5 mile you traverse beneath pyramidal Rose Knob, then in another 0.5 mile reach a junction. You are now about 9.8 miles from the Brockway Summit trailhead. Here the old Western States Trail forks left, goes 30 yards to the ridgeline, follows its sometimes snowy north-facing slopes 0.25 mile east, then makes a meandering, moderate descent 0.6 mile northeast down to clear, but knee-deep Gray Lake, which has excellent campsites above its north shore. The TRT, however, stays high and continues straight ahead, east across south-facing slopes toward Rose Knob Peak (9710 feet), an impressive pile of volcanic rock with three distinct pointy peaks. After a 0.5 mile traverse across slopes, the TRT crosses a saddle with clusters of whitebark pines, then soon climbs 0.25 mile southeast, where it passes beneath the southernmost summit of Rose Knob Peak. Then the trail rounds the bend and travels northeast across talus on the south-facing side of the mountain.

This rocky section was one of the last parts of the trail to be completed, and one of the most difficult to build. The trail builders have constructed formidable rock walls and created a fairly smooth trail through the talus field. As you go around the mountain you will once again enjoy magnificent views of almost the entire lake. After a 0.3-mile traverse across mostly talus, the trail angles north and contours over to a saddle above Mud Lake; this stretch has a few scattered mountain hemlocks. At the east edge of the saddle is a junction, about 11.2 miles from the Brockway Summit trailhead and 7.7 miles from the Mt. Rose trailhead. (See sidetrip "Gray Lake.")

From the saddle between Mud Lake and Gray Lake, the Tahoe Rim Trail goes right (southeast) and descends gently 0.25 mile on an open slope above Mud Lake, with additional spectacular views all the way to Fallen Leaf Lake at the far end of Lake Tahoe, in the distance to the south. The TRT then traverses 0.25 mile northeast, exchanging a volcanic trail tread for a granite one (shortly to be followed by another volcanic one briefly before returning to a granitic one). You reach a junction from where the now abandoned Western States Trail descends across private property, and so should be avoided. About 50 feet below this junction, near some willows, is a small spring that can provide water for most of the season. After the snow melts, this is your last source for water until you get to a pond at the intersection of the TRT and Mt. Rose Trail, about 5 miles away.

With 7.2 miles remaining, start up the TRT on a series of short switchbacks. You soon traverse just below a dramatic large red and black volcanic rock at the top of a ridge. The trail passes just below and to the east of this rock and climbs slightly to the north-facing side of the mountain about 0.75 mile past the junction. Below is Ginny Lake, and in the distance Tahoe Meadows, the Mt. Rose Highway, and Mt. Rose itself. You now traverse slightly uphill across the north-facing slope to a saddle just below a granite ridge. Here you have crossed a steep slope that will be covered in snow for most of the year. Take care if the pathway is icy. The terrain is spectacular with several large craggy volcanic rocks towering above and a hemlock forest below.

SIDETRIP **Gray Lake**

To the left (north) of the TRT, the old Western States Trail makes a steep downhill grade of about 0.5 mile to Gray Lake,. You can access the lake via this trailhead or the one about a mile back. Why not visit Mud Lake, which is just below us to the right? Here's why: Mud Lake lives up to its name. In late summer it gets quite small before sometimes disappearing altogether. Gray Lake may be the only lake easily accessible and worth visiting on this section of trail. A charming streamlet lined with wildflowers drops down through the rocks into the southern edge of the lake, and then pours out of the north facing side of the lake. While in early- and mid-summer the lake can be a haven for mosquitoes, in the fall it is a pleasant and quiet place to relax. At 9043 feet this lake with marshy surroundings is quite fragile so take extra care to not damage the plants near the lake. Look for good flat campsites in the forest on the north shore of the lake. Note the especially large lodgepole, whitebark pines, and hemlocks in this idyllic setting. While it's not great for swimming, as the only dependable lake between Watson Lake and Star Lake, Gray Lake is well worth a stop.

At the saddle, you now face your second 800-foot climb; the first was up to the wilderness boundary below Mt. Baldy. The imposing massif straight ahead would be formidable if you tackled it head-on, but fortunately the TRT does not, and the climb is exceptionally well-graded. From the saddle the TRT has several short switchbacks up among granite boulders, and then it jogs east, then west. Here, it climbs 0.6 mile north and has abundant views, to a switchback just above the east end of a west-trending ridge that climbs to the summit of Relay Peak. Along this ascent, Clark's nutcrackers flit between the scattered gnarled whitebark and western white pines. From the switchback, huge panoramic views open up to the west of Castle Peak, Donner Lake and the Truckee area, and to the south in the distance, Freel Peak above Lake Tahoe. From your vantage point you also have closer views: west down the gaping West Fork Gray Creek Canyon, and a close-up view of the nearby Slab Cliffs, northwest down equally gaping Gray Creek Canyon, and northeast to a radio-towered peak.

From this switchback, which can lie under snow well into July, you are about halfway up your major ascent. The TRT climbs 0.5 mile southeast up volcanic slopes, and you surpass 10,000 feet in elevation before you reach a switchback that has poor views. You now have two shorter switchback legs to Relay Peak, the highest point on the entire Tahoe Rim Trail at 10,338 feet in elevation. On a clear day you can see all the way to Lassen Peak and, rumor has it, Mt. Shasta if the day is crystal clear. The panorama seems unlimited as dozens of narrow valleys and ridgelines unfold before you. Much of what you see in the foreground is the Mt. Rose Wilderness. You may see burned trees several ridgetops away providing evidence of the 15,000-acre Martis Fire of June 2001. You also see Mt. Rose (10,776 feet) standing out to the northeast in its full volcanic relief. At sunset, the mountain certainly lives up to its name as it takes on a beautiful rosy hue. Finally, to the east-southeast, beyond Tahoe Meadows and Ophir Creek canyon, lies large Washoe Lake.

From Relay Peak your trail now merges with an old aban-

Mt. Rose from Relay Peak

doned dirt road that heads downhill steeply north along the ridgeline to a relay microwave tower developed by AT&T. While the top of the ridgeline provides an excellent location for receiving radio waves, it is unfortunate to see a large ugly tower in this incredibly beautiful location. Near the tower you reach a junction with a broad gravel road, which is still used by vehicles for administrative purposes.

You are now leaving the wilderness, and mountain biking is allowed over the 3.9 miles between here and Highway 431 (Mt. Rose Highway). Now you begin a journey down to the Mt. Rose Highway on the dirt road. As noted earlier, eventually the Tahoe Rim Trail Association will be able to replace this long journey on a utility road with a trail between the Mt. Rose Trail and the radio tower. With the beautiful terrain in this bowl, a well-developed trail which switchbacks its way up to Relay Peak will be impressive.

On this broad utility road you first descend 0.3 mile south to a switchback, then 0.5 mile northward to a bend east, where you pass an old chair-lift. Before the road to the top of the ridge was built, this chair-lift was constructed as a means to bring the building materials necessary for the relay tower to the top of the mountain; later the lift was used to access the tower during extreme winter periods when snowcats were unable to make the trip to the top. The road descends into a big open bowl with scattered stunted whitebark pine trees. In the winter this area is popular with skiers, snowshoers, and snowmobilers. Now after 1.4 miles of moderately steep downhill on the road, you reach a small pond, known both as Snow Pond (because it is covered in snow much of the year) and as Frog Pond (See sidetrip "Mt. Rose.")

At the pond if you are a hiker you have two choices, both of which are the Tahoe Rim Trail. If you're on a bike or a horse you have only one choice: to go straight ahead on the old TRT route 2.5 miles to the trailhead. The new TRT goes left and follows the old Mt. Rose Trail.

Route One: The Old TRT: You follow the old road straight ahead on a usually gentle descent, the first half south, the second east. About 1 mile past the pond you get full views of Incline Lake, Lake Tahoe, and Tahoe Meadows. Far below, the next section of the TRT can look like a brown snake wandering through the deep green of Tahoe Meadows. The views remain panoramic and inspiring as the road continues gently downhill to a junction with a single track trail at about 2.1 miles from the Snow Pond. Here the TRT turns left and traverses gently uphill to the Mt. Rose Summit trailhead. (If you stay on the dirt road straight ahead you

SIDETRIP **Mt. Rose**

Mt. Rose is 1700 feet of climbing, much of it above the treeline, from the TRT/Mt. Rose Trail junction. If you are up for a good climb it is worth it as the views along the way and at the top are extraordinary. Mt. Rose is unique in several ways, and has a superb "garden" of alpine plants. One's the woody fruited evening primrose, which is found almost exclusively on its slopes. This low-lying plant produces one or more large yellow blossoms on short stalks close to the ground. The flowers, which are pollinated by nocturnal moths and then die shortly afterward, smell like coconuts. Mt. Rose also seems to have its own weather pattern. Often you can hike in shorts and a short-sleeve shirt until the last 0.5 mile, where you encounter fierce winds and chilling temperatures. During a major winter blizzard the top of Mt. Rose is truly frightening. The easiest way to the top of Mt. Rose is to start at the Mt. Rose/TRT trailhead, which makes for a 10-mile round trip with just under 2000 feet of climbing.

will quickly reach Highway 431, where you can turn left and go 0.3 mile to the Mt. Rose Summit trailhead, or turn right and go 0.4 mile to the Tahoe Meadows trailhead.)

Route Two: The new TRT: You hike briefly uphill and then begin a 0.7 mile descent on the Mt. Rose Trail/TRT to a junction. You first pass through a meadow, and then begin a fairly steep descent past several wildflower fields and near a creek before crossing the creek and meeting a junction. From here a left turn takes you uphill to the summit of Mt. Rose, the Tahoe area's third highest peak, in 2.6 miles.

From the TRT/Mt. Rose trail junction, your TRT heads to the right and downhill, quickly crossing the creek again. This luscious bit of moisture may be the first supply of clean water you have seen in miles and miles, and the nearby environs make for some nice camping spots (although on a weekend it will be quite crowded as the trail to Mt. Rose is one of the most popular day hikes in the area). In just a hundred yards or so you cross another little stream and pass just below Galena Falls, a delightful waterfall cascading down just above the trail. The falls are a real highlight of this section of trail. Follow a short use trail to the falls' base to get your feet wet and cold. The TRT now circles above a large meadow and heads on a gently rising traverse below the slopes of beautiful, volcanic Tamarack Peak. The well laid out trail passes awesome views of Mt. Rose and Tamarack Lake. At about 2 miles from the junction with the Mt. Rose Trail, a wide panorama of Lake Tahoe and Tahoe Meadows opens up before a gentle downhill traverse to the Mt. Rose Summit trailhead. This new trailhead facility is located at the very top of the Mt. Rose Highway, across the street from the Mt. Rose Campground. It has pit toilets and parking. Thru-hikers can cross the highway to the campground and then hike an almost level 0.8 mile on the Tahoe Meadows Interpretative Trail to the Tahoe Meadows trailhead.

Tahoe Meadows to Spooner Summit

(23.1 miles)

Difficulty—This section is strenuous, mostly due to the length, but also because of elevation gains. While the trail starts at 8740 feet and ends at about 7140 feet, there are two portions of the trail where you encounter climbs of over 700 feet. In the opposite direction, the climb from Spooner Summit to just below Snow Valley Peak is about 1800 feet.

Best Seasons—It is best to hike this section of the trail between mid-June and late October. The segment between Spooner Summit and Snow Valley Peak may be open as early as mid-May in years with light snowfall. However, the section between Twin Lakes and Snow Valley Peak may hold snow well into July.

Highlights—There are spectacular vistas of Lake Tahoe along much of this section of trail. Some of these are the most stunning views to be found anywhere along the Tahoe Rim Trail. In particular, the Christopher's Loop (Herlan Peak) spur trail offers especially remarkable vistas. The trail provides views on both sides of this north-south oriented ridge, of Lake Tahoe to the west, and of the Great Basin to the east. While the thin decomposed granite soils along the trail limit wildflower growth, in several locations flowers can be found in abundance. This is especially the case if you take a sidetrip down to Marlette Lake, where the wildflower display is one of the best to be found anywhere. If you are looking for yellow and orange aspen leaves, it is hard to beat the bounty of leaves at Snow Valley, Marlette Lake, and Spooner Lake. Much of this section of trail can be covered on a mountain bike, and, for the experienced rider, affords some of the best mountain biking at Lake Tahoe. This section of trail is home to the Tahoe Rim Trail 50Km/50Mile/

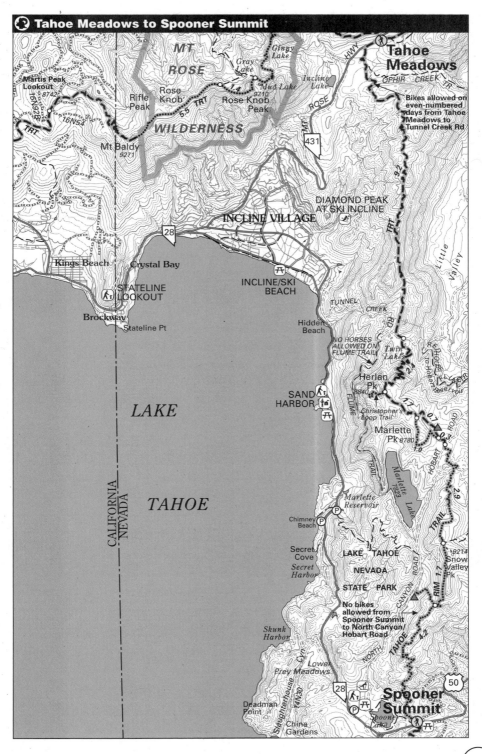

MT
ROSE

Ginny
Lake

Gray
Lake

Mud Lake
9710

Incline
Lake

Martis Peak
Lookout
8742

Rose
Knob

Rifle
Peak

Rose Knob
Peak

1.4

5.5 TRT

TRT

16N92B

16N54

WILDERNESS

Mt Baldy
9271

HWY

OPHIR   CREEK

**Tahoe
Meadows**

**Bikes allowed on
even-numbered
days from Tahoe
Meadows to
Tunnel Creek Rd**

431

MT   ROSE

TRT   3.2

DIAMOND PEAK
AT SKI INCLINE

INCLINE VILLAGE

28

Little

Valley

Kings Beach   **Crystal Bay**

**STATELINE
LOOKOUT**

Brockway

Stateline Pt

Hidden
Beach

**INCLINE/SKI
BEACH**

TUNNEL   CREEK

RD

Twin
Lake

LAKE

TAHOE

CALIFORNIA
NEVADA

NO HORSES
ALLOWED ON
FLUME TRAIL

**Herlan
Pk**
8840

Rd Passes
to Hobart

2.4

1.3

0.7

**SAND
HARBOR**

FLUME

**Marlette
Pk** 8780

Christopher's
Loop Trail

1.0

0.3

HOBART   ROAD

TRAIL

Marlette
Lake
7823

2.9

**Marlette
Reservoir**

Chimney
Beach

P

P

**Secret
Cove**

Secret
Harbor

LAKE   TAHOE

NEVADA

STATE   PARK

1.1

9214

**Snow
Valley
Pk**

RIM   1.7

**Skunk
Harbor**

**No bikes
allowed from
Spooner Summit
to North Canyon/
Hobart Road**

CYN

CANYON   ROAD

TAHOE   RIM   TRAIL

NORTH

4.2

**Deadman
Point**

Lower
Prey Meadows

Steighenhouse

14N30

28

China
Gardens

50

**Spooner
Summit**

P

Spooner
Lake

100Mile run that occurs in July. As their slogan says, it truly is a glimpse of heaven and a taste of hell. For more information go to www.tahoemtnmilers.org.

Heads Up!—Very little water is available on this section of trail. Bring some along for Fido. About 0.7 mile beyond the Tahoe Meadows trailhead, you cross Ophir Creek, a beautiful little stream. At around mile 3 you pass two unreliable seasonal springs. At about 9.5 miles from the trailhead you reach the Twin Lakes. These two small lakes may dry up by late in the summer; as they shrink, the water becomes less attractive, and takes on a green hue. Another source for water is Spooner Lake, near Spooner Summit. If you're thru-hiking you should know that there are no trailside sources of water on the next 12 miles south of Spooner Summit. Obtain water at Spooner Lake unless you have made prior arrangements for water to be provided to you. While Spooner Lake's water itself looks marshy, you can also walk over to the Spooner Lake parking lot above the lake. Here you will find tapwater and, during the summer months, the small store sells ice cream, snacks, and drinks. You will see Marlette Lake from the trail. If you are thirsty and/or looking for a swim, it may be a worthwhile detour. From the intersection of the TRT and Hobart Road, it is 1.75 miles to the lake, mostly steep downhill. About 0.75 mile down, where two gullies converge, there is a usually reliable stream. This may be a good source for water if you are camping at the Marlette Campground, which is about 1 mile from the stream.

Most of the trail is exposed to the sun and wind so bring extra water, extra clothing and lots of sunscreen. Camping is only allowed in two locations: One site, Marlette Peak Campground, is along the TRT near Marlette Peak, about 13 miles south of the Mt. Rose trailhead; the second campsite is along North Canyon Road. While Marlette Campground does not have a source for water, the TRTA has been leaving bottles of water at the campground, and requests a donation to meet expenses. At a minor saddle, just before you reach Snow Valley Peak, take a dirt

Marlette Lake and Lake Tahoe from near Snow Valley Peak

road 1.2 mile steeply down to North Canyon Road. Turn left and go about 1 mile south down to North Canyon Campground, just east above the road. All you will see is an outhouse, with camping sites behind it out of view from the road. Get water from the stream just to the west of the road. You can also continue on the TRT, past Snow Valley Peak an additional 1.7 miles, to a signed junction with a connector trail, which heads downhill 1.4 miles to the campground.

Tips for Mountain Bikers—For the experienced mountain biker this section of trail is perhaps the finest section on the entire Tahoe Rim Trail. It is best to ride from north to south. The Forest Service has ruled that mountain bikers should only use the northernmost 9.2 miles of this section of trail (from Mt. Rose Highway to Tunnel Creek Road) on even days of the month so that hikers may experience the trail without bikers on the odd days of the month. On an even weekend day in the middle of the summer, be prepared to see as many as 100 bikes. After an initial fun ride across the meadow and then along the old Ophir Creek Trail, you turn right and climb to a saddle. Then it is a wonderful, sometimes challenging ride, mostly downhill, for the next 8 miles to Tunnel Creek Road. The trail is sandy and soft in some sections, but in most places it is firm and a real pleasure to ride. Some will feel challenged by portions of the trail; for most, the trouble is well rewarded. At Tunnel Creek Road you can turn right and ride downhill 3 miles to Highway 28 where you can have a shuttle awaiting you. Or you can cross the road and head a short distance to Twin Lakes. The next few miles after Twin Lakes are a challenging steep uphill ride, but well worth the effort since they eventually lead to spectacular views of Marlette Lake and Lake Tahoe. When you reach Hobart Road, turn right. Bikes are not allowed on the rest of this section of the TRT. Hobart Road takes you down to Marlette Lake, where you follow North Canyon Road out to the parking lot at Lake Tahoe Nevada State Park, where fees are required for parking, or for riding through the park.

Getting There, Highway 431 (Mt. Rose Highway) to Spooner Summit—The trailhead is located 7.3 miles north on Highway 431 (toward Reno) from the Highway 28 and 431 junction in Incline Village. You will drive past Tahoe Meadows on your right to a parking area and restroom facility on your right. The trail starts from the western edge of the lower parking lot. From Reno, this trailhead is found about 0.75 mile after the highway tops the Mt. Rose Summit.

Getting There, Spooner Summit to Highway 431 (Mt. Rose Highway)—From Tahoe City you travel 27 miles east on Highway 28 to reach the junction with Highway 50. Turn left on Highway 50 and drive 0.7 mile to the trailhead on the north (left) side of the road (approximately 14 miles northeast of South Lake Tahoe on Highway 50). There is a small dirt parking area on the north side of the highway, situated across from a larger paved parking lot, which provides access to the southbound TRT. It is important to realize that Spooner Summit is not the same as Spooner Lake. Spooner Lake is about 0.5 mile west of the junction of Highways

Sand Harbor from Christopher's Loop

50 and 28 on Highway 28. Entrance to the popular Spooner Lake area (with access to The Flume Trail) requires a fee, and is reached by driving 0.6 mile northwest from the junction.

Trail Description

From Highway 431, known locally as the Mt. Rose Highway, the southbound TRT runs parallel to the highway and descends past several streamlets and then crosses through the middle of Tahoe Meadows, a large subalpine area that can be muddy in June or a wonderful wildflower tromp in July. Stay on the trail to avoid damaging the fragile meadow ecosystem. Near the south edge of the meadow, cross Ophir Creek, a charming year-round stream that is bordered by elephant heads, lupines, and other wildflowers. Except for the fact that you just left the trailhead 0.75 mile back it would be the best source for water on this section of trail. After crossing Ophir Creek, the trail heads into a forest of lodgepole and whitebark pines, and meets the Ophir Creek Trail, where you turn left (south).

For the next 0.2 mile, you are on a smooth, wide trail, walking past lodgepole pines. Soon to the left you see Tahoe Meadows and the radio towers atop Slide Mountain, before the trail meets a junction at 1 mile from the trailhead.

Straight ahead is the Ophir Creek Trail. It starts out level in the lodgepole forest and then heads downhill, sometimes steeply, past prolific groves of aspen trees and western white pines to the backside of Slide Mountain.

In 3 miles you reach what remains of Upper Price Lake, which was significantly reduced in size by a landslide in 1983. This is a great trail for fall colors and to see how Slide Mountain got its name. It also seems to be a very popular area for hang gliders. One beautiful fall day I sat mesmerized by the antics of eight gliders riding the thermals above Slide Mountain. Eventually you reach Davis Creek County Park in 7 miles, although most will find the venture to Upper Price Lake and back a better way to spend their time.

The TRT turns right and starts a gentle climb south up the sandy surface past more scattered lodgepole pines, and occasional western white pines and whitebark pines. Exposed to high winds and heavy snows on this north-facing slope, the trees are smaller than those you will see later on the south-facing side of the ridge. To the north you can see the rose-colored top of Mt. Rose.

At 1.7 miles from the trailhead you reach a saddle, about 250 feet above the Ophir Creek Trail. Here you get your first views of Lake Tahoe through the vegetation. The views will just keep getting better and better as the miles go by. Now your pathway is along a long north-south oriented ridge for the next 7.5 miles, going in and out of the tops of east-west oriented gullies. Along the route you will experience numerous gentle ups and downs, and from the saddle will have an overall drop in altitude of about 900 feet to Tunnel Creek Road.

The first mile past the saddle is a gentle, sandy contour along the western slope of the ridge. You pass scattered white granite boulders, appearing as if they were tossed there haphazardly by

Looking south from Christopher's Loop

a giant playing with rocks. Lodgepole pines are now fewer and larger, and some impressively large western white pines are seen with their long narrow cones hanging from the top. Some may mistake the western white pines for sugar pines, but the sugar pine cones are quite a bit larger, and sugar pines are usually found at lower elevations. At 2.5 miles from the trailhead you cross the head of a gully; here the trail changes from its eastern direction to a southern direction. You see a wide view of the lake, looking toward Emerald Bay and Mt. Tallac. Several large, flat granite boulders lie just below the trail making this a great spot to sit and enjoy the views.

Next you ascend gently and enjoy more views of the lake looking toward the Nevada/California border, which lies on a large peninsula jutting straight south into the lake. Soon, about 3 miles from the trailhead, you reach two spring-fed streamlets and colorful lush vegetation which provide a cool break from the dry, sandy terrain that surrounds the area. The trail next winds up and down past a few hemlock trees before reaching another saddle at 3.6 miles from the trailhead with views of Mt. Rose to the north. You then begin a short moderately steep descent over a number of evenly spaced granite steps (a joy for the experienced mountain biker), followed by a short climb to another viewpoint.

Every half mile you walk provides an even wider and more beautiful view of the lake. On a clear windy day, the wind ripples shimmer in the sun as the lake turns a deep blue. At a little more than 4 miles from the trailhead, your trail now crosses to the east-facing side of the ridge, passing a flat opening with stumps from ancient logging. Here you get your first glimpse of Washoe Lake and the Great Basin to the east. A gentle descent leads to a wider opening with a view of all of Washoe Lake.

At 4.6 miles from your Tahoe Meadows trailhead you go southwest, gently uphill, followed by a moderate descent, back to the west-facing slope. Here where the trail takes a sharp left turn, you find another viewpoint just off the trail to your right. Again, several flat boulders provide a resting spot to appreciate the views. Southwest across Lake Tahoe you see Twin Peaks (8878 feet), prominent above the northwest shore, and to the southwest, Emerald Bay and behind it, Maggies Peaks (8699 feet and 8499 feet). Incline Village lies directly below you to the west.

Past this viewpoint you travel into a thicker forest of red firs and scattered western white pines as you cross to the east-facing side of the ridge once again. Soon, you reach a trail hanging on the edge of the steep bank and pass just to the east of the top of a Diamond Peak Ski Area lift, before reaching a saddle at 5.7 miles from the trailhead. Here you find wide, open, east-facing views toward Carson City and Washoe Lake. The trail next bends to the west and Lake Tahoe so dominates your senses that it appears as if you could walk right into it. Jeffrey pines now predominate, as you head down a short, steep rock staircase (many bikers will want to get off their bikes, others will wish they had half-way down). The long ridge that includes Mt. Baldy, Rose Knob Peak, and Relay Peak can be seen to your north. Below you to the west are the ski runs and condominium developments of Diamond Peak Ski Area, the town of Incline Village, and the Incline area golf courses.

About 1 mile past the Diamond Peak ski lift, the trail climbs through granite boulders to the eastern slope again. Here you pass from the land of Jeffrey pines to the land of red firs, and meander up and down gently through the forest before reaching another viewpoint opening through the trees to the east. About 7 miles from your trailhead, you start a moderate descent on a long switchback. If you are hiking, you will enjoy views to the east of Little Valley and Washoe Lake. If you are on a bike, you will be hanging on, trying not to lose your balance on the deep, soft sand. From the bottom of the descent, you pass ground-hugging pine-mat manzanita and chinquapin, before briefly heading through a fir forest, and then back out into a mostly treeless west-facing slope, about 8 miles into your hike.

The final stage of your journey to Tunnel Creek Road is a gentle up and down through a moderately dense forest of red and white firs on a trail cut out of the side of the ridge. Views of the lake are mostly filtered, with one last dramatic viewpoint to the west toward the beaches of Incline Village, Twin Peaks, Dollar Point, and the Lake Forest "island" (a peninsula during low water periods, an island during high water periods). Highway 267 can be seen climbing over the top of Brockway Summit.

At Tunnel Creek Road, 9.2 miles from your trailhead, you meet a junction with the Red House Flume Trail. Now you are in a very busy mountain biking area for much of the year. If you are hiking, keep your eyes open for riders; if you are riding, watch out for hikers. (See sidetrip "Flume Trail.")

To continue on the Tahoe Rim Trail, go straight through level terrain about 0.3 mile to the lower of the two Twin Lakes. These lakes have been the location of several

SIDETRIP Flume Trail

A left turn here soon takes you downhill steeply on the Red House Flume Trail, a popular bike loop in combination with the Flume Trail. A right turn takes you downhill steeply for 0.5 mile to a junction with the Flume Trail. From this junction, a left turn will take you on the Flume Trail (although it is recommended that you ride the Flume Trail the opposite direction, starting from Spooner Lake), a right turn goes down Tunnel Creek Road steeply for 2.6 miles to Highway 28.

backcountry camps sponsored by mountain biking groups and the Tahoe Rim Trail Association who use the camps as they work to maintain and improve the trail. These shallow grass-lined lakes may dry up by mid-summer after a dry winter. If you're desperate for water, the higher of the Twin Lakes, not visible from the trail, dries up later than the lower lake.

From the east shore of Lower Twin Lake, you face a 1.5-mile long, 750-foot climb, usually moderate, but sometimes steep, through the mixed forest of pine and fir trees. With the soft sand surface, this trail will feel steeper on a bike than if you are hiking. There are occasional views of Mt. Rose back to the north and Lake Tahoe to the west. After a series of switchbacks, you almost reach the top of Peak 8706. Traverse west below it, then go south downhill into a level open area, before traversing briefly west and climbing again. This climb is shorter, a mere 0.25 mile, and just before leveling off, you reach a junction at about 2.4 miles from the trail intersection with Tunnel Creek Road. This is the Christopher's Loop spur view trail on Herlan Peak. If you are on your bike leave it here as bikes are not allowed on this viewpoint loop. (See sidetrip "Christopher's Loop Trail.")

You are now about half way through the TRT's Section 3. Heading southeast on the TRT you will find that the route has leveled off before it enters an area that is thick with hemlock trees, which can hold the snow until early summer. A short distance farther, you pass through a flat area of scattered pine trees before

SIDETRIP Christopher's Loop Trail

This 1.2-mile loop trail is well worth the climb. The trail switchbacks steeply up to the top of a sandy ridge. Now you are at the top, but the best viewpoint is still a bit of a walk west toward the lake. Your trail goes across an open plateau and in a fairly short distance reaches Christopher's Loop. You can go either right or left, as both routes will take you to the viewpoint. Once you are there, you are standing on a granite cliff looking down on Sand Harbor while the entire lake unfolds before you. It is the best view of Lake Tahoe I have seen anywhere. The first time you see it, your jaw will drop in amazement. The view to the south of Marlette Lake and Snow Valley Peak is also spectacular. This is a great spot to stop for lunch, although at about 12 miles from the trailhead, it will take a very early start, or a bike, to get here by lunch time.

Christopher's Loop

reaching a wide open treeless ridgetop. Here, about 0.75 mile beyond Christopher's Loop, walk about 100 yards south on a use
trail, which ends with inspiring views of most of Marlette Lake
in the foreground, and Lake Tahoe in the background. Nearby,
Marlette Peak and Snow Valley Peak are visible to the south.

The trail now heads east and down to the eastern slope of the
ridge to an area thick with some especially large lupine and paintbrush plants. Stop and gaze to the east for another view over the
flowers to the Great Basin. When you continue, you will descend
along the east-facing slope past grassy areas with more wildflowers and forested areas of red fir and hemlock. This is a wonder-
fully enjoyable rolling stretch on a mountain bike. You meet a
trail junction at 1.7 miles from the Christopher's Loop junction.
From here you have two alternative TRT routes to choose from.
The trail to the right is for hikers only; in 1 mile it traverses the
west and south slopes of Marlette Peak, providing panoramic full
views of Marlette Lake, Snow Valley Peak, and Lake Tahoe. A left
turn at the junction keeps you on the Tahoe Rim Trail, which
continues to be multiple use here. You head through more roll-

ing forested terrain and in 0.5 mile, meet the simple Marlette Peak campground with pit toilet and a few picnic tables. While no water source is available at the campground, the TRTA provides bottled water at the campground and requests a donation to cover the costs. If you're planning on camping at Marlette Peak, contact the TRTA in advance to be sure water is currently available. Just 0.2 mile farther it meets the trail which circled Marlette Peak, and the trails are rejoined as one. So which route should you take? If you are bike riding, please only ride on the bike (east) section. If you are a hiker and would enjoy more sensational views, take the slightly longer (by 0.3 mile) Marlette Peak Trail.

From where your trails meet, you head 0.3 mile mostly down-

SIDETRIP **Marlette Lake**

If you need water or would enjoy a swim in a wonderful lake, or if you are on a mountain bike, leave the Tahoe Rim Trail and turn right on Hobart Road and head 2.1 miles down to a junction by the southeast shore of Marlette Lake, named after Seneca Hope Marlette, the first Surveyor General of California and one of Tahoe's first mapmakers. Mountain bikes are not allowed on the remaining portion of this section of the TRT, so you must turn right if you are biking. Hobart Road is level for about 0.5 mile and then heads downhill steeply over some very soft decomposed granite to a flatter section of great riding past springtime wildflowers and aspen trees to the junction next to Marlette Lake. The east shore of Marlette Lake in the spring or early summer has one of the most prolific exhibits of wildflowers anywhere. Over 50 different species of flowers are reported to be in this area including lupine, paintbrush, monkshood, horsemint, columbine, tiger lily, and elephant heads.

From the junction, a short road descends to the southeast shore of Marlette Lake, where you can stop and swim and then continue south on the main road on your left, which heads 0.7 mile to the top of the saddle. From the saddle, follow North Canyon Road, the next 3.9 miles of hard-packed sand down to the Spooner Lake parking lot. On a bike this is a fun downhill, but watch out for hikers and be sure to obey the speed limits. Yes, speed limits! (5 miles per hour on turns or when passing someone, 20 miles per hour maximum anywhere else.) If you are walking, bound for Spooner Lake via North Canyon and wish to avoid the bikers, take the new Marlette Lake Trail, where bikes are not allowed. It starts on the south end of the lake, near the main creek that drains into the lake, and heads 4.5 miles to the Spooner Lake parking lot. Along the trail you will enjoy beautiful views of Snow Valley and Snow Valley Peak, lots of aspens, several streams, and the remains of a logger's cabin. Next to the beginning of the Marlette Trail is a fish spawning station. To see the fish in action visit this spot in June or early July.

Marlette Lake and Lake Tahoe

hill through open sandy terrain to a junction with Hobart Road. At this junction, several alternatives are available to you:

At the Hobart Road junction, which is about 14.3 miles from the Tahoe Meadows trailhead, and about 8.8 miles from the Spooner Summit trailhead, the TRT crosses the road and begins the 2.9-mile journey to the saddle below Snow Valley Peak, the ascent with a 700-foot climb. Bikes are not allowed between Hobart Road and Spooner Summit on the Tahoe Rim Trail. Head initially east into the trees and soon begin a moderate ascent south. After about 0.7 mile, the TRT reaches a jeep road and follows it about 140 yards west before turning south again. If you are low on water, take this road 0.2 mile southwest down a gully to where the road starts a climb northwest. Continue about 200 yards down the gully to a spring. Beyond the jeep road your ascent gets steep as you journey through a forest of red firs and western white pines. You see occasional glimpses of Snow Valley Peak to the south, and of Marlette Lake to your west. As you near the top of the ridge and Snow Valley Peak, there are fewer trees (a few windblown whitebark pines) and the views are more spectacular. You pass through expansive fields of lupine and sagebrush bordered by piles of granite rock boulders. To the north, you can see downtown Reno and its surrounding desert as well as Mt. Rose. Just before reaching the saddle below Snow Valley Peak, the trail crosses to the west-facing side of the ridge, providing unobstructed views of Marlette Lake and Lake Tahoe. This makes for a wonderful spot for lunch or rest before beginning the long descent to Spooner Summit. At a shallow notch by the northwest base of Snow Valley Peak, the TRT crosses a dirt road coming up from North Canyon below (the large valley and meadow area to the southwest). (See sidetrip "Spooner Lake.")

From the junction of the TRT and this dirt road you can also climb in 0.3 mile to the top of Snow Valley Peak, at 9214 feet the highest peak on the eastern slope of the Tahoe basin. To get there just follow the road east as it climbs up the mountain. The walk to the top of Snow Valley Peak requires an additional 270 feet of climbing for a view that to my mind is not as good as the one of Marlette Lake and Lake Tahoe you just passed. Ah, but peak baggers will have bagged a peak.

SIDETRIP Spooner Lake

To go to Spooner Lake, turn right and in 1.2 miles of steep downhill you will reach a spring and then immediately North Canyon Road, where you turn left. From here, an additional 3.8 miles of a moderate, then gentle, downhill path will take you to Spooner Lake at the Lake Tahoe Nevada State Park's parking area. Remember, that is Spooner Lake, not the Spooner *Summit* trailhead parking lot for the Tahoe Rim Trail. When you arrive at North Canyon Road after coming down from Snow Valley Peak, you could also take the Marlette Lake Trail to Spooner Lake or Marlette Lake. Cross the road and hike about 50 yards west to the Marlette Lake trail. To go to Marlette Lake, turn right and go downhill about 0.5 mile to the lake. To go to Spooner Lake, turn left and go about 3 miles moderately steeply downhill to a junction with North Canyon Road. Cross the road and follow the pathway another 0.5 mile to the Spooner Lake parking lot and nearby lake.

If you stay on the Rim Trail heading south, you will hike 5.9 miles from the junction with the dirt road to the trailhead at Spooner Summit. The first mile is a rambling gentle downhill across an exposed ridge with sagebrush, tobacco brush, lots of granite boulders, and a few stunted whitebark pines. You get expansive views of Lake Tahoe, as well as views of the North Canyon

Road and a vast forest of aspen trees. The view is especially spectacular in the fall with a sea of yellow aspen leaves. Enjoy the open view because soon you will be in a dense forest. If you have a pair of binoculars, you can count the numerous bikers grunting their way up the steep North Canyon route toward Marlette Lake, and the ever popular Flume Trail.

The Spooner Lake Cross-Country Ski Area operates here in the winter, maintaining groomed trails that head up from Spooner Lake to Marlette Lake, Hobart Road, and depending upon snow conditions, to the top of Snow Valley Peak. In addition, Spooner Lake Outdoor Company owns and operates several very charming log cabins close to the Tahoe Rim Trail that are available for rental year round, as well as a shuttle service for mountain bikers and hikers using the Flume Trail or the Tahoe Rim Trail. For more information contact Spooner Lake Outdoor Company at (775) 749-5349, or at www.theflumetrail.com.

After an abundance of Lake Tahoe views, the trail ventures to the east-facing side of the ridge for views of Eagle Valley, with its sprawling Carson City. Then you head into a thick forest of red fir and Jeffrey pine as the trail continues down the ridge. Along this ridgeline section, as you may have seen earlier on the trail, are old weathered stumps cut as high as 5 to 6 feet off the ground. These trees were cut in the 1870s providing wood for the Marlette Flume below Marlette Lake, from where the wood traveled by water to Carson City, and eventually Virginia City, to support the silver mines. The dry climate of the east shore has kept the trees from further decomposition over all these years. At 1.7 miles from the junction with the trail to the top of Snow Valley Peak, you meet a junction on a minor crest saddle. From here, a trail descends northwest, losing over 700 feet in elevation as it switchbacks in 1.4 miles to the primitive North Canyon Campground and the adjacent North Canyon Road. Near this campground, water can be found at a small creek that flows through a grove of aspens just west of the road.

On the TRT, with a little over 4 miles to go, your trail now winds gently downhill along a heavily forested ridgeline of pine and fir trees. The trail is soft dirt and an easy walk (although if you are doing this whole route in one day, it may not seem easy at this point). Occasional filtered views open up, but this is primarily a walk through a shady forest. At 1.4 miles south of the campground trail junction, a vista trail leads off to the right. After a 100-yard jaunt up this spur trail you will find views of Lake Tahoe and the mountains above the lake's west shore. If you started hiking from the Spooner Summit trailhead, this vista point is 2.8 miles from the trailhead, and 1000 feet above it.

Your gentle-to-moderate walk winds through the forest pathway for another 2.25 miles before ending with a short steep descent to a dirt road. On it the TRT turns left, and you walk 0.5 mile, passing a large grove of aspen trees with filtered views of Spooner Lake, to the end of the section.

Alternative Routes

Do you like the beautiful views, but are not quite ready for a 23-mile jaunt? Take a look at some of these alternative routes that provide for a shorter trip.

- Start at the Tahoe Meadows trailhead and hike as far as you want and then turn around. You will find an abundance of great viewpoints and numerous lunch spots on the flat granite rocks. This relatively easy trip makes an excellent route for children.

- Start at Tahoe Meadows and hike 9.2 miles south to where the TRT runs into Tunnel Creek Road. Turn right (west) and walk or ride steeply downhill for 3.1 miles to Highway 28. Be careful on the downhill as the sand can be quite deep, especially later in the summer and fall. If you time it correctly the fall colors in Tunnel Creek canyon can be spectacular. Shuttle service may be available through Spooner Lake Outdoor Company at (775) 749-5349.

• Start at the Spooner North Trailhead and hike 5.9 miles to the saddle below Snow Valley Peak where you meet a dirt road. Turn left and follow this road 1.2 miles to where it intersects the North Canyon Road. Turn left again and walk 3.8 miles to the Spooner Lake parking lot. You can then walk around Spooner Lake and find a trail to the Spooner Summit parking area.

SECTION 4

Spooner Summit to Kingsbury Grade

(13 miles)

Difficulty—Moderately difficult. There is a steady climb of about 1600 feet in the first 5 miles, and a wonderful almost level mile in the middle, filled with views. Then the trail is mostly downhill. The starting elevation is 7150 feet, and the ending elevation is 7780 feet, with the high point just a little below the top of South Camp Peak (8866 feet). This is the easiest section of the Tahoe Rim Trail to hike, particularly in the opposite direction, with just over 1000 feet of elevation gain.

Best Seasons—Early June to late October. As on most of the east shore, the snow melts faster here than on the west shore. There are several heavily forested north-facing sections that may retain snow until late June, but in most areas the snow melts by late May.

Highlights—The biggest highlight of this section is the spectacular view of most of Lake Tahoe, and the west shore, from South Camp Peak. This unobstructed view looks directly up the entrance of Emerald Bay to the mountains of Desolation Wilderness. At South Camp Peak you will find lots of rocks to sit on, and even a wood bench that some kind trail builder provided. This could be the perfect TRT lunch spot, especially since it is about halfway between Spooner Summit and the Kingsbury trailhead. Making South Camp Peak your turn-around point for an out-and-back hike or ride makes good sense whether you are starting from the Spooner Summit trailhead or from Kingsbury Grade.

Heads Up!—Water is not available on this section of trail. Be sure to bring plenty of water for yourself and your pets. If you are thru-hiking be sure to fill your water containers at Spooner Lake before you reach the trailhead. While South Camp Peak itself might

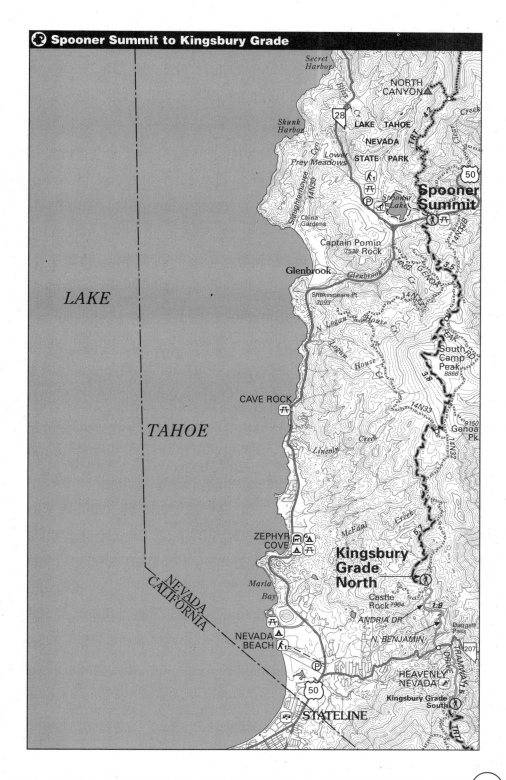

Secret Harbor

NORTH CANYON▲

BISS Cr.

TRT 42

Creek

28

LAKE TAHOE

50

Skunk Harbor

NEVADA

STATE PARK

Lower Prey Meadows

Slaughterhouse Cyn

14N30

Spooner Lake

Spooner Summit

14N32B

China Gardens

Captain Pomin
7538 Rock

PEAK GENOA Cr.

3.5

Glenbrook

Glenbrook

Shakespeare Pt
7093

14N32A

LAKE

N. Logan House

Logan House Cr.

PEAK

South RD
Camp
Peak
8866

3.8

TAHOE

CAVE ROCK

14N33

14N32

9150
Genoa
Pk

Lincoln

Creek

McFaul

Creek

5.1

ZEPHYR COVE

**Kingsbury
Grade
North**

Marla
Bay

Castle
Rock 7904

1.9

ANDRIA DR

Daggett
Pass

NEVADA
BEACH

N. BENJAMIN

TRAMWAY S.

207

NEVADA
CALIFORNIA

P

HEAVENLY
NEVADA

50

Kingsbury Grade
South

TRT

STATELINE

make a good camping spot, the lack of water makes this hike best for dayhikes. Much of the trail is open and exposed to the sun so be sure to bring plenty of sunscreen. If you are hiking, watch out for mountain bikers, because this is a popular biking trail. If you are biking, watch out for hikers, because it's also popular with hikers. Both groups should watch out for horses.

Tips for Mountain Bikers—Mountain bikes are allowed on this entire section. This ride can be completed from either direction, with the impressive views of South Camp Peak in the middle making a good location for a break. The section from Spooner to South Camp Peak is a great ride. It is an easy-to-moderate climb most of the way on smooth and sandy trails. If you get to the top and turn around, the downhill is a thrill, fun but not too difficult. The section from South Camp Peak to Kingsbury is more technical due to rocky steps and challenging terrain.

Getting There, Spooner Summit to Kingsbury—From the "Y" in Tahoe City drive 27 miles east on Highway 28 past Incline Village to the top of Spooner Summit, where Highway 28 meets Highway 50. Turn left on Highway 50 and drive 0.7 mile to the trailhead parking lot on the right, which has room for 20 cars. Your Spooner-to-Kingsbury trailhead has a pit toilet and several picnic tables in a nice setting under a grove of aspen trees. The trailhead is about 14 miles northeast of South Lake Tahoe on Highway 50. Directly across Highway 50 is the Spooner-to-Highway 431 trailhead.

Getting There, Kingsbury to Spooner Summit—From Highway 50 at Stateline, Nevada drive 2.9 miles up (east) Highway 207 (Kingsbury Grade) and turn left on North Benjamin Drive. (This is 0.3 mile before the top of Daggett Pass). North Benjamin becomes Andria Drive, and you go a total of 1.9 miles from the highway to the end of the pavement and a trailhead with the Tahoe Rim Trail sign on your left.

Looking toward Emerald Bay from South Camp Peak.

Note: As this edition goes to press, the Tahoe Rim Trail Association is planning to begin construction on a trail between the Kingsbury North and Kingsbury South trailheads. Currently you walk over 3 miles on roads and cross a major highway to get between the trailheads. The new trail will not only avoid the drudgery of this road walk, but will give the hiker and other trail users new spectacular views, and a few miles of new trail to discover. It will also provide access to the TRT via the Henry Van Sickle Park just above the casinos in South Lake Tahoe. Check with the TRTA for the latest on trailhead locations and details.

Trail Description

From Spooner Summit, the mostly sandy trail climbs moderately up a somewhat open slope where manzanita, chinquapin, tobacco brush, and sagebrush grow. In a fairly short time, the grade eases and you begin a steady, but less steep, climb through open forest, meadows, and thicker stands of Jeffrey pines and red firs. Here, the trail is smooth, hard-packed sand, which is wonderful for mountain bikers. This open forest is a popular area for both deer and bear, and at least one mountain lion has been spotted in the area. During the drought period of the early 1990s, a high percentage of trees in the area died because they lacked the necessary moisture to fight off invading bark beetles. In the late 1990s the area was logged heavily to remove the dead trees. The result has been a more open forest and some new dramatic views of the surrounding mountains.

Along the way south toward South Camp Peak, you intermittently glimpse Lake Tahoe and Desolation Wilderness to the west, and Snow Valley Peak to the north. Mule ears, paintbrush, lupine and several aspen groves grow along the trail. After about 550 feet of ascent and 1.5 miles, you reach a little knoll with a short spur trail to the top, providing views into the Carson Valley and to the north toward Snow Valley Peak (9214 feet) and Mt. Rose (10,776 feet), two mountains of the Carson Range. While enjoying the view, contemplate the Carson Range, which is the transition zone between two very different environments. To the west, along the slopes above the western edge of Lake Tahoe, is the heart of the Sierra Nevada, where every winter copious amounts of snow fall. That area is lush with a thick forest, green meadows and countless lakes. The snow lasts well into summer. Where you stand in the Carson Range, on the other hand, receives about half as much snow as the western slope. The trees are more scattered and lakes are rare. The dryer area that you see to the east, begins the basin and range high desert zone, which dominates most of Nevada and Utah. This area receives considerably less annual precipitation than the Carson Range. While many factors determine what the natural surroundings look like, in the western United States the biggest determining factor is how much precipitation an area receives.

About 0.6 mile past the spur trail your route turns from south to east, and after a nearly level 0.4-mile traverse, it crosses a minor road about 250 yards north of where it ends at Genoa Peak Road,

Genoa Peak from South Camp Peak

a major forest service road. A large aspen grove grows alongside it, but you won't find any flowing water. You've climbed only about 100 feet in the last mile, but now you turn southward and climb gently 0.4 mile to an abandoned road that would take you southeast in 0.25 mile to a pond that usually has water into June. After a second 0.4-mile climb, you reach a second short spur trail, which takes you to less spectacular views. Now you descend 0.3 mile west to a crossing of the major Genoa Peak Road, about 3.5 miles from the trailhead, adjacent to a large open staging area for logging operations. The trail then becomes increasingly steeper as you begin an unrelenting 800-foot climb to the crest of South Camp Peak through heavily forested terrain. You may see signs of logging, including numerous blackened stumps. The trees were cut down and the brush and debris from them was burned. Just before reaching the northwest edge of South Camp Peak, the trail passes through a thickly forested north-facing section where you may see some early summer snow.

South Camp Peak is a large, nearly level, open area with great picnic sites. You walk along the broad summit's west rim; and, its low-lying shrubs do not obstruct the spectacular views, which you have for 1 mile. The summit in fact is so broad and level that "Peak" is certainly a misnomer. The highest rock outcropping is about 0.75 mile along your rim traverse, and looking southeast from it, you see, Genoa Peak, the pointy nearby peak with a radio tower on top. Scanning clockwise, next you see Heavenly Ski Resort and beyond it to the south, the brown, rounded Freel Peak; Stateline, and its casinos, as well as the rest of the South Lake Tahoe area; evidence of the Angora Fire of 2007; Fallen Leaf Lake; Desolation Wilderness, including the pointy spire of Pyramid Peak; Mt. Tallac, which seems to rise up right from the lake; Emerald Bay and evidence of the landslide that occurred in 1955, just after the construction of Highway 89 along the bay. Next comes Stony Ridge, with Jacks Peak and the nipple-topped Rubicon Peak, and then to the west the deep westshore canyons: Blackwood, and Ward (with Twin Peaks on the ridge between the two canyons). Increasingly northwest you see Alpine Meadows, Squaw Valley, and to their north, Castle Peak above Donner Summit. While the views are spectacular, sometimes the winds are ferocious as you gaze from this exposed lookout straight into prevailing westerly winds. From this angle you can see right into Emerald Bay and you may get the mistaken impression that Lake Tahoe is 100 miles long and 5 miles wide. Unless you take a steep sidetrip up to Genoa Peak, this is the highest elevation point along this section of trail, at around 8800 feet elevation. If you would like to hike an out-and-back on this section of the TRT, this is the place to turn around. It makes for a wonderful 10- to 12-mile round trip (mileage depending on where you turn around). About midway along the journey across the open area of South Camp Peak, you may discover the small abandoned and caved-in copper mine. This site may be dangerous so avoid exploring.

If you complete the entire point-to-point route from Spooner Summit to Kingsbury Grade, you will probably drag yourself away from the views and start heading gently downhill and away from the sometimes stiff winds in the direction of Genoa Peak. In 0.5 mile you reach a saddle with a dirt road that climbs southeast to Genoa Peak. (See sidetrip "Genoa Peak.")

On the TRT, from the junction with the Genoa Peak jeep road, you begin a 5.7-mile long and usually gentle descent toward Kingsbury Grade. The forest here is composed primarily of small young Jeffrey pines, red firs, and

> **SIDETRIP Genoa Peak**
>
> In 0.8 mile of steep climbing you will be at the top of Genoa Peak (9150 feet). The views of Lake Tahoe from the top of Genoa Peak are similar to those from South Camp Peak, but you get the added bonus of views of Carson Valley to the east. On the negative side, you will be standing next to a radio tower. The area around Genoa Peak is popular with glider planes. Once, I saw one fly by so near to the peak that the pilot and I were close enough to wave to each other.

western white pines, and you may continue to see the blackened stumps left behind by past logging. Pinemat manzanita, a luscious green groundcover, is especially prolific in this section and adds a nice green feel to the hike. About 0.7 mile past the road which led up to Genoa Peak, you cross a small dirt road on the floor of a gully, and here the trail turns northwest and then south as it rounds a peak. You traverse the mountainside on a trail that has become more challenging and technical for mountain bikers. Your path is now bordered by granite boulders and has many rock steps to climb over. The forest has become thicker so you can only get an occasional glimpse of the lake. One of these views, however, is a dramatic look at Emerald Bay and Mt. Tallac, which feels much closer to this section of trail. As you continue on a more narrow, rocky trail, you see Heavenly Ski Resort and its accompanying development. The stark view of high-rise condominiums detracts from the feeling that you are away from it all.

The last mile of the trail rolls up and down along short stretches. Just 0.5 mile shy of the finish, a short vista trail heads off to your right. While the views from the vista point are not nearly as lovely as the views you saw earlier, this vista makes for a pleasant short hike to a viewpoint from the Kingsbury Grade trailhead.

Past the viewpoint your trail curves east and soon terminates at the end of a paved road.

To get to the next section of the TRT you must walk 1.9 miles to Highway 207 on a paved residential road, and then an additional 1.5 miles on the other side of the highway to arrive at the trailhead under the Stagecoach chair-lift at Heavenly Valley. About 0.8 mile north of Highway 207, thru-trekkers can obtain water at George Brautovitch Park, along the road's west side.

SECTION 5

Kingsbury Grade to Big Meadow

(23.2 miles)

Difficulty—This long and relatively strenuous section has a lot of elevation changes, and a 9730-foot high point. While a trail of this length is too long for many to hike in one day, for the strong hiker it is a wonderful dayhike.

Best Seasons—Each end of the trail can be hiked as early as mid-June. The highest part of the trail near Freel Peak is usually not open until mid-July or later, depending upon the amount of snow received the previous winter. The first major snows at Freel Peak may come as early as the middle of October.

Highlights—This trail section provides tremendous views of Lake Tahoe, Carson Valley, Desolation Wilderness and the Carson Range. In addition, it has a wonderful high-elevation lake, Star Lake, and access to the summit of the two highest peaks in the Tahoe basin: Freel (10,881 feet) and Jobs Sister (10,823 feet).

Heads Up!—Some sections of the trail are above 9000 feet in elevation, and much of the trail is open and exposed to the sun and wind—bring your sunscreen. As with all sections of the trail along the east shore of Lake Tahoe, water is in short supply. In the first few miles out from the Stagecoach parking lot, there are several seasonal streams, with the South Fork of Daggett Creek lasting the longest. Star Lake, which you will reach at 8.8 miles from the Kingsbury trailhead, is a beautiful source of water. About 1 mile past Star Lake you find a stream coming down from Freel Peak, a tributary of Cold Creek. On slopes west of Freel Peak, several small streams cascade across the trail into late summer. From Armstrong Pass you may find water by heading southeast from the TRT on the steep Armstrong Pass connector trail. It is 0.4 mile long, and

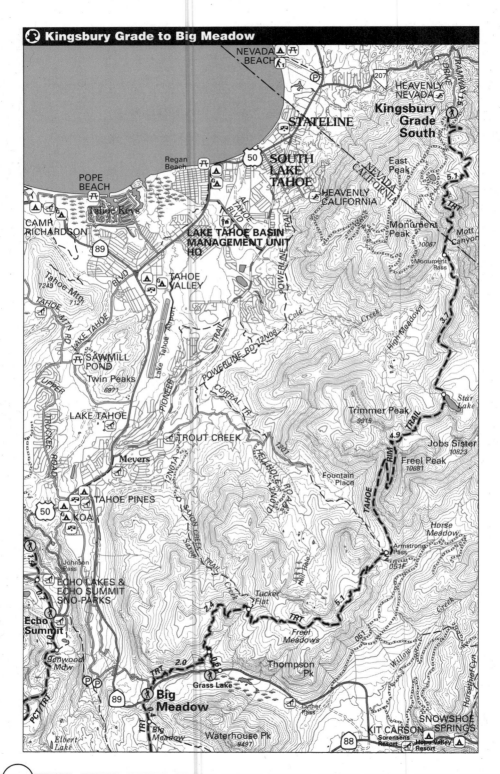

near its bottom you cross a small stream. From its trailhead a dirt road descends almost 0.5 mile to cross larger Willow Creek. You can find reliable water just below the west edge of the western Freel Meadow. Finally, east of the Big Meadow trailhead, there is Grass Lake Creek, a major stream, at approximately 0.5 mile, and another one at 2 miles from the trailhead at the Grass Lake Trail junction.

Tips for Mountain Bikers—This section is challenging, loved by some and hated by others. It has lots of technical areas with hundreds of rock benches that will require many riders to dismount. Portions of the trail are along steep drops that may unnerve some riders. The first portion is primarily a long steady climb, with the exception of a brief steep downhill on some very sandy, loose soil. Once you get to the top of Monument Pass, just about when you are wondering why you are doing this, the trail levels off for some great riding for several miles to Star Lake. After Star Lake it is a major, difficult climb again up to 9700 feet. Almost everyone will be walking his or her bike near the top. From the saddle of Freel Peak, it is time for a big downhill with a few tight little switchbacks that may scare some riders. Eventually, you reach Armstrong Pass, a great place to escape if you have had enough. A short trail descends to a dirt road, Forest Route 051F, that you can follow 0.5 mile down to Forest Route 051 and take it 3.5 miles to Highway 89. If you do this, you will reach Highway 89 0.8 mile east of signed Luther Pass, and 1.8 miles above the Highway 88/89 junction in Hope Valley. If you continue toward Big Meadow, you will confront another long uphill, followed by another long downhill. Along the downhill section, you pass the junction to the Saxon Creek Trail. This very popular mountain biking trail, usually accessed via the Big Meadow trailhead, is known as Mr. Toad's Wild Ride. While some may find it a wild ride, I found it to be very chewed up and steep and impossible to navigate in many sections. If you go, be prepared for difficulty. Past "Mr. Toad's" is a brief steep uphill, followed by a steady

Freel Peak

downhill to the end of the trail, which is fun, but not without several technically challenging sections.

Getting There, Kingsbury South Trailhead to Big Meadow Trailhead—From Stateline in the South Lake Tahoe area drive east up Highway 207 (Kingsbury Grade) 3.2 miles to Tramway Drive at Daggett Pass, the summit of Kingsbury Grade. Follow the signs 1.5 miles to the Heavenly Valley Resort Stagecoach parking lot. Look for the Tahoe Rim Trail sign at the south end of the parking lot underneath the Stagecoach chairlift.

Getting There, Big Meadow Trailhead to Kingsbury South Trailhead—From the intersection of Highway 89 and Highway 50 in Meyers, drive 5.3 miles south on Highway 89 to the Big Meadow Trailhead and parking area, on your left. Luther Pass is 3.3 miles farther on. This trail can also be accessed from the Grass Lake trailhead, which you will find by driving south on Highway 89 past the Big Meadow trailhead for 1.5 miles. Park on the right side of the road in a roadside pullout and cross the highway to the trail. If you pass Grass Lake, the lake that looks like a meadow on the right, you have gone too far.

Note: As this edition goes to press the Tahoe Rim Trail Association is planning to begin construction on a trail between the Kingsbury North and Kingsbury South trailheads. Currently you travel over 3 miles on roads and cross a major highway to get between the trailheads. The new trail will not only avoid the drudgery of the road walk, but will give the hiker or rider new spectacular views and a few miles of new trail to discover. It was also provide access to the TRT via the Henry Van Sickle Park just above the casinos in South Lake Tahoe. Check with the TRTA for the latest on trailhead locations and details on this trail section.

Trail Description

Amidst high-rise condominiums and a huge parking lot, the trailhead is located underneath a ski lift. Are we talking a wilderness experience here or what? Don't worry, it gets better. You start with a 0.3-mile, very steep climb to a saddle, where you cross under the Stagecoach ski lift. Up here you go 80 yards south on a road to the trail's resumption, which immediately turns east. The trail switchbacks moderately up through a forest of red firs and Jeffrey pines and provides views of the condos below and later brief glimpses of Lake Tahoe and Washoe Valley. You walk over numerous granite boulders and steps, which are challenging to those on bikes.

After climbing for close to 1 mile you reach a saddle and then descend gently for 0.5 mile, passing under another Heavenly Ski Resort ski lift. In another 130 yards you cross the South Fork of Daggett Creek, which runs most of the year. It provides a patch of greenery and wildflowers amongst the thick brown forest. As you ascend again, western white pines and lodgepole pines replace the red firs and Jeffrey pines.

Next the trail gently climbs through alternating areas of dense forest and a more open combination of brush and forest with manzanita and tobacco brush dominating the scene. The open vegetation allows views east to Carson Valley and desert ranges beyond it. About 0.75 mile past the creek you reach the north rim of Mott Canyon, where you see Freel Peak. You follow the rim for a 0.5-mile moderate ascent west, then climb gently 0.25 mile south to where, about 3.3 miles from the trailhead, you reach a saddle and a ski area maintenance road. You drop very steeply, but thankfully briefly, on this road over soft sandy soil (careful on your bike!) into Mott Canyon. Just underneath the Mott Canyon chair-lift, is beautiful little Mott Canyon Creek. In the early summer, its banks are covered with Lewis monkeyflower, yellow monkeyflower, delphinium, and columbine. The lovely stream runs most of the season, but may dry up by late summer. If you are hiking this section in late summer or fall, the South Fork of Daggett Creek will be your water source between the trailhead and Star Lake.

After a short distance with a moderate climb, you come out of Mott Canyon and round the corner to an open traverse. Your route is now mostly treeless and facing east with stunning views of Carson Valley far below to the east and Jobs Sister, with its huge drop in elevation from mountain top to valley floor, in the distance to the south. To your left, and steeply below, is evidence of a major forest fire reaching up toward Jobs Sister from the Carson Valley. Here you will see mountain mahogany and the largest western white pine I have ever come upon just to the left side of the trail. With a circumference of 24 feet, the pine provides shade in this hot, exposed section of trail. While beautiful to hike, anyone who is afraid of heights will find this cliff-edge section of trail a challenging bike ride, which becomes steeper toward Monument Pass.

Approximately 5 miles from the trailhead, you climb to Monument Pass, which is crossed by powerlines, and which is about 0.4 mile beyond the Nevada-California boundary. At the pass you cross from the Carson side (eastern slope) to the Tahoe side on the western slope. Monument Peak at over 10,000 feet is

Star Lake

a towering presence to the west. Dramatic views of Jobs Sister and Freel Peak immediately open up.

It is 3.7 miles from Monument Pass to Star Lake. The first 2 miles are on a gentle, sandy path through mostly open terrain, and provide a wonderful opportunity to marvel at the views of Desolation Wilderness, including Pyramid Peak and the Crystal Range, and Lake Tahoe to the west. The results of the Angora Fire come clearly into view. This fire in the summer of 2007 burned over 3000 acres and 250 homes near South Lake Tahoe. As you get closer to Star Lake, the immense size of the Freel Peak massif becomes more and more impressive. A little over 1 mile before Star Lake, the trail begins to ascend again, sometimes moderately, and the tree cover of western white pine, lodgepole, and hemlock gets thicker. Finally you reach Star Lake, located at the base of Jobs Sister, which rises dramatically from its shores. This alluring lake will take your breath away, especially if you venture into its cold waters (although after an extended warm period the water temperatures can become quite bearable). As the only large lake on the Tahoe Rim Trail between Mt. Rose and Luther Pass, this may be the best place to set up camp for those who are doing an overnight trip. There are several overused camping spots close to the lake and lots of wonderful camping spots above the lake.

When you leave Star Lake, the trail can be a bit confusing; just follow the rocky pathway over the lake's outlet. The first mile or so after Star Lake is to me the most interesting mile of this section of the TRT. You begin with a moderate climb from Star Lake, with good views of Lake Tahoe. You are now in the wide open at a high altitude where western white pines, whitebark pines, and hemlocks are scattered amongst the sandy soil. Many of the trees have been tortured by high-altitude winds and are stunted and bent. You also see numerous large pieces of white quartz along this section as well as patches of snow that hang on late into the summer. You head steadily toward 10,000 feet in elevation, passing an early summer waterfall and then viewing the imposing hulk of Freel Peak. You will arrive at a swiftly moving clear mountain stream, a tributary of Cold Creek. Only a foot or two wide, it creates a green grassy path through the desolate sand and rock.

SIDETRIP Freel Peak

At this saddle, you can begin a steep climb to the top of Freel Peak, at 10,881 feet the tallest peak on the Tahoe-basin rim. A recently built trail switchbacks up the steep slope, climbing 1150 feet in elevation in a mile to the top of the peak. From Freel Peak you can easily hike cross-country over to the top of Jobs Sister (10,823 feet). Climbing these peaks makes challenging, but beautiful, jaunts if you are camping in the Star Lake area, and of course the views are spectacular.

If you head upstream, you will find open terrain, good for camping. As you reach the saddle below Freel Peak, at the high point of 9730 feet, don't be surprised to find a patch of snow even in late July. This often windswept spot is about 1.9 miles south of Star Lake and 3.0 miles north of Armstrong Pass. (See sidetrip "Freel Peak.")

Those who find over 23 miles just about enough to hike, can skip Freel Peak and continue on the TRT. Here you are almost midway through Section 5, about 10.7 miles south of the Kingsbury South trailhead, and about 12.5 miles north of the Big Meadow trailhead. Your trail begins with a long steady thinly forested descent 0.7 mile south to a switchback, which turns you back to the north. You continue downhill for an additional 0.3 mile before switching back again to the south. Once again, you will enjoy excellent views of the Crystal Range, the massive granite ridge on the western edge of Desolation Wilderness. You soon cross three spring-fed creeks that are usually flowing and provide much-needed water and beautiful wildflower displays. These little ribbons of color in this dry, brown landscape are a welcome relief. Less than 0.5 mile past the last streamlet is a huge mass of granite with a steep cliff face and lots of fascinating rock formations known as Fountain Face, about 1 mile north of Armstrong Pass.

> **A Tale of Two Fountains**
>
> The Fountain Place you see on the map is a meadow area, below to the west. Both Fountain Face and Fountain Place were named for Garret Fountain, who built a way station at Fountain Place in 1860 in an effort to supply miners on their way from California to the Comstock Lode in Nevada. Fountain hoped they would go over Armstrong Pass, but instead they chose Daggett Pass, and Fountain's dream failed.

Less than 0.3 mile before Armstrong Pass the trail is gently graded; you experience a gentle up and down traverse, and pass many large juniper trees, with their light blue berries and gnarled trunks and branches, along the way.

At the deep crest notch of Armstrong Pass, you can leave the TRT to shorten your hike. (Or, if you come in from Armstrong Pass, it makes for a relatively short way to access Freel Peak.) The short, steep Armstrong Pass Trail takes you 0.4 mile to an old abandoned road. Follow this road 0.5 mile to trailhead parking just across a small bridge. From here it is 3.4 miles to Highway 89 and about 5 miles to Hope Valley. Follow the Armstrong Pass trailhead directions below in reverse. (See sidetrip "Armstrong Pass.")

The Armstrong Pass junction is located at the top of the "U" shaped valley at the end of the long southward traverse. Here, the trail rounds a corner of the ridge and heads west. From Armstrong Pass, the journey to Big Meadow is 9.5 miles. In just 0.1 mile you reach a junction with a trail that descends northwest toward Fountain Place and Oneidas Street. This trail is another access to

To access Armstrong Pass from Highway 89 (a section of road recommended only for 4-wheel-drive vehicles with high clearances), take Highway 89, south from the junction of Highway 89 and Highway 50 in Meyers up to signed Luther Pass, just beyond a large grassy meadow holding Grass Lake. Start on a long downhill toward Hope Valley going 0.8 mile to a junction with Forest Service Road 051 on your left. (This junction is 1.8 miles up from the Highway 88 junction down in Hope Valley.) Take this road steeply uphill. In 1.1 miles the road divides. There is a gate on the right fork, but stay left. At 1.6 miles, bear left. At 1.8 miles, you cross a cattle guard, then continue to bear left. At 2.4 miles, you reach your first bridge as you follow a stream. At 2.7 miles, at a fork in the road, go straight ahead. At 3.4 miles, you will reach the second bridge; cross this bridge, then immediately make a 180-degree left turn into a small parking area. Park here and then walk across a trail bridge and go 0.5 mile uphill on the now abandoned road to the Armstrong Pass connector trail. Take this trail 0.4 mile steeply uphill to the junction with the TRT.

the TRT from South Lake Tahoe. The TRT quickly leaves the ridge to begin this next phase with a steady, sometimes steep uphill climb on sandy soils through a forest of scattered western white pine, lodgepole pine, and red fir. Your views are now fewer and less dramatic with occasional glimpses of the Freel massif to your northeast as you switchback up the ridgeline past some large trees. The area between Big Meadow and Armstrong Pass is popular for mountain biking. If you are on your bike, enjoy, but watch out for hikers. Be a little more vigilant if you are hiking. While portions of this section are a fun sandy ride, there are a lot of short rocky sections that will force many riders to get off their bikes; other sections are composed of deep granite gravel that will make it tough, whether you are going up or down. After 2 miles of switchbacking uphill, you reach an open, broad ridge with large boulders and with views to the south of numerous peaks above 10,000 feet, including Round Top near Carson Pass at 10,381 feet.

The trail soon leaves the ridge and proceeds through a rocky area with stone steps, then it continues through an open forest until, at a little less than 3 miles from Armstrong Pass, you traverse the largest of three meadows known as Freel Meadows. USGS maps show this area as Freel Meadows, but are not specific

Star Lake

as to how many meadows are included. I found three meadow-like areas within 1.5 miles. The first "meadow" is open slopes dotted with mule ears, lupine, and paintbrush which slopes away from the trail (the actual meadow lies at the base of the slopes). Beautiful Sierra peaks can be seen to the south. Just past the open slopes, you reach an excellent viewpoint to the north. Here you see deep, boggy, Hell Hole Canyon directly below you, and farther in the distance to the north, Lake Tahoe. To the northeast, Freel Peak stands out in full relief. Next, you pass through an open forest before reaching a large grassy meadow to your left (the second meadow). Then shortly you reach a third meadow, this one loaded with wildflowers, including corn lily, lupine, and delphinium. You can get water from the west end of this meadow, at the headwaters of Saxon Creek. The Freel Meadows area is a wonderful green divide between the more barren sandy slopes of the higher elevations to the east, and the thick forest that appears after the meadows.

After leaving this meadow, you descend at a moderate pace through denser forest. About 1 mile later, and 5.1 miles from Armstrong Pass, you reach the Saxon Creek Trail (alias "Mr. Toad's Wild Ride") on a broad saddle just above Tucker Flat.

With 4.4 miles left, you continue on the TRT over a short up-hill section northwest, followed by a short traverse west, then you have 2 miles of meandering downhill through primarily dense forest of red and white firs and western white and Jeffrey pines, until you reach the Grass Lake Trail. Along the way you see several small meadows with many wildflowers, especially mule ears. There are also two viewing spots. The first is near the top on a very short use trail to a rock outcropping with views to the northwest of Lake Tahoe. The second viewpoint is after the trail switchbacks down through the forest to another rock outcropping on the east side of the ridge. Here you have views of the mountains to the east and southeast. A special visual treat is a small creek that you cross, shaded by lush aspen trees that pop out of a jumble of huge granite boulders.

SIDETRIP "Mr. Toad's Wild Ride"

This popular mountain biking trail is usually accessed via the Big Meadow Trailhead, and is known as Mr. Toad's Wild Ride. If you start at Big Meadow, this ride starts with a long uphill followed by a big challenging downhill. Before you ride this section, be sure to read the mountain biking tips at the beginning of this chapter. This trail is recommended for expert riders only.

At 2.0 miles from the Big Meadow trailhead, you meet the Grass Lake Trail, an alternative TRT route to Highway 89. On the Grass Lake Trail, you can hike only 0.6 mile to meet Highway 89, which is 1.4 miles less of walking or riding distance (and 400 feet of ascent or descent) than on the trail to the Big Meadows trailhead. If you are heading to the Grass Lake trailhead you will find a moderately steep downhill through the trees to the trailhead located next to Highway 89. You have now had the pleasure of being on the first section of the Tahoe Rim Trail, which was built by the Tahoe Rim Trail Association in 1984.

A small but reliable stream can be found near the junction of the Grass Lake connector and the Tahoe Rim Trail. There is only one more water source to be found, Grass Lake Creek, in the next 1.6 miles, about 0.4 mile from the end of the trail. That is a larger stream and a good source for water. If you continue to the Big Meadow trailhead, you will journey through more of the same terrain, a gentle downhill on many switchbacks through a mostly thick forest of predominantly Jeffrey pine and red fir. While Highway 89 cannot be seen from the trail, it can often be heard. At the finish, you will arrive at a paved road, on which you turn left and go 100 yards to the entrance to a large parking lot and restroom facility (no water). At this junction you can turn right and find an overflow campground with toilet, trash receptacles, food storage lockers and tent sites just 0.25 mile down the paved road. The next section of the TRT heads up to Big Meadow, Round Lake and eventually the Pacific Crest Trail and can be found past the trailhead restrooms at the southwest corner of the parking lot.

SECTION 6

Big Meadow Trailhead to Echo Summit/Echo Lake

(15.3 miles to Echo Summit, 17.5 miles to Echo Lake)

Difficulty—This section is moderately strenuous. Most of the trail is gentle up and down terrain or almost level through meadows or open fields. While there are several sustained climbs, they are not too steep and most will find this section of the TRT not exceptionally difficult. The most difficult portion of the trail is between Bryan Meadow and Benwood Meadow, where you will experience an almost continuous, steep descent (or a steep climb if coming from Echo Summit).

Best Seasons—This section of trail is best hiked from late June to early October. While you may see a few snow patches well into July, the trail is mostly snow-free by late June. The wildflowers come into full bloom in late July or early August, which makes that the best time to hike this section. When those flowers are in bloom you are in for an incredible treat.

Highlights—There are three beautiful lakes on this trip: Round Lake is only a 5.2-mile round trip from the trailhead. Dardanelles is 1.4 miles off the TRT and provides a 6.8-mile round trip. Showers Lake is a good half-way stop at 7 miles into the 15-mile hike (18 miles if you also go to Dardanelles Lake). You will find impressive volcanic rock formations jutting high above the shores of Round Lake, and on the ridges above Meiss Meadows. There are two large meadows, Big Meadow and Meiss Meadows, which if you come at the right time of year, will provide you with some of the most stunning displays of wildflowers you will see on the Rim Trail. In addition, other interesting flora is found on the trail, including some spectacular juniper trees. At a wonderful

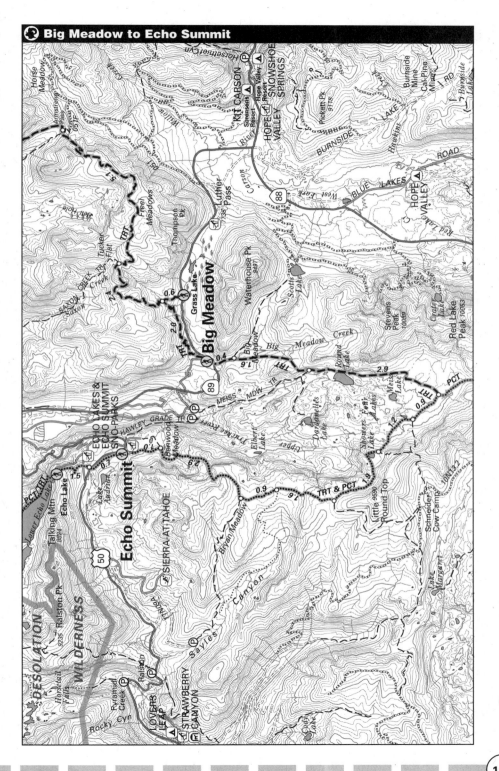

large bowl just past Showers Lake, you will encounter waterfalls and numerous wildflower-bordered streams caused by springtime snow melt, and spectacular castle-like volcanic rock formations. This section may have the greatest variety of views and habitats of any section of the TRT.

Heads Up!—While the trail has several good water sources and places to swim, the second half of the trail, between Showers Lake and Echo Summit, has more limited water supplies, especially in the fall. Water can be found at the following locations: About 0.7 mile south of the Big Meadow trailhead in Big Meadow is Big Meadow Creek, which may dry up in the fall. The Upper Truckee River in Meiss Meadows is usually a swift-flowing stream. About half way through the hike is Showers Lake, an excellent water source.

The 2 miles of the trail descending to Benwood Meadow are quite steep, which can be very hard on the knees and every other body part. From the Echo Summit end, this is a major uphill starting just 1 mile into your hike.

Tips for Mountain Bikers—From the Big Meadow Trailhead bikes are allowed on the first 5 miles to the junction of the Tahoe Rim Trail and the Pacific Crest Trail. Bikes are not allowed on the Pacific Crest Trail, so this ride is a 10-mile out and back. Much of this ride is technically challenging, with lots of rocks, but for experienced riders it can be a fun ride.

Getting There, Big Meadow to Echo Summit—From the intersection of Highway 89 and Highway 50 in Meyers (south of South Lake Tahoe) drive 5.3 miles south on Highway 89 to the Big Meadow Trailhead on your left (this is about 3.3 miles before signed Luther Pass). The previous segment from Kingsbury Grade to Big Meadow trailhead ends here, and you start across the road and head uphill toward Big Meadow. The trailhead has a restroom facility and informational kiosks.

Castle formations north of Showers Lake

Getting There, Echo Summit to Big Meadow—Drive west on Highway 50 from South Lake Tahoe to the top of Echo Summit (4 miles west of the intersection of Highways 89 and 50 in Meyers). Just 0.3 mile past Echo Summit make a left turn, which is marked with an Echo Summit Sno-Park sign. Park on the southern end of the parking lot, and find the trail just to the west.

Trail Description

The trail starts out at the lowest point in the Big Meadow Trailhead parking lot (southwest end). You walk about 250 yards through a forest of white fir, Jeffrey pine, and juniper before you cross Highway 89. Once you cross the road the trail starts south. It is moderately steep, taking you uphill over rocky terrain through a thicker forest of Jeffrey pine, western white pine, and fir. After a little more than 0.2 mile you pass to the left of Big Meadow Creek, its bed filled with huge granite boulders and lined with aspen trees. By 0.3 mile from the trailhead the grade moderates, becoming almost level as you walk close to a stream on the right surrounded in the fall by the yellow leaves of aspen trees. Stop and shut your eyes and listen to the quaking sound that gives the aspen its name. Soon you reach a junction. A left turn here would take you to Scotts Lake. Your trail, however, continues straight ahead to a large flat meadow with the new and original name of "Big Meadow." Just as you enter the meadow, the trail crosses a stream, which is good sized in the spring, but may dry up in late summer. This is, of course, Big Meadow Creek. As you head south across the meadow you are treated to views of the surrounding mountains to your southwest. At only 0.7 mile from the trailhead, you can reach the meadow in half an hour and enjoy a wonderful setting.

After you cross the meadow, the trail heads uphill again through the fairly dense forest of lodgepole, western white pine, and red fir. The tree cover thins out as you reach more open and sunny areas with sagebrush and a variety of wildflowers including lupine, mule ears, and pennyroyal. You now occasionally pass small groves of aspen trees. About 1 mile past the meadow you reach a saddle, and head 0.25 mile downhill on a steep section of trail that affords you great mountain views to the south and west. At 2 miles from the trailhead you reach a junction. To your right, the Meiss Meadows Trail (Christmas Valley on the sign) will take you toward Dardanelles Lake in 1.4 miles. (See sidetrip "Dardanelles Lake.")

On the TRT you continue straight ahead and begin a gentle ascent through some very interesting volcanic rock mudflow formations. At 2.6 miles from

SIDETRIP Dardanelles Lake

To reach Dardanelles Lake, you descend northwest on the Meiss Meadows Trail for 0.2 mile through a mixed forest of pine, fir, and a few junipers, to another trail which you take; you will hike an additional 1.2 miles on it to Dardanelles Lake. The trail first crosses a creek, then levels off in a grassy meadow before it climbs again up a rocky tread. You reach Dardanelles Lake on a big granite flat that overlooks the lake. Above the lake's south shore is a massive rock cliff reaching right down to the water. There are great camping spots at Dardanelles Lake above a large flat expanse of granite that reaches down to the northeast shore of the lake. The midsummer water can be warm in this beautiful lake so enjoy a swim and then bask on the granite slab. Ah . . . now you know why you put that backpack on. Be forewarned, however; at only 3.4 miles from the trailhead you are not likely to be swimming alone.

the trailhead (and 0.6 mile from the last junction), you reach the northeast corner of Round Lake. Round Lake is the largest lake you will encounter on this section of trail, and makes for great swimming and camping. The best campsite is at the lake's northwest corner by the outlet, but the lake can get crowded on a sunny summer weekend. Thanks to an influx of volcanic sediments, Round Lake's color varies from a brownish-green to an unusual aqua-blue, more reminiscent of the lakes and streams of western Canada than most of the lakes in the Sierra. As you walk past Round Lake, a spectacular steep cliff of volcanic rock reaches skyward on your left. Known as the Dardanelles, you will have the pleasure of gazing at this fascinating rock formation from several locations as you complete your hike.

Just past Round Lake you pass a small seasonal stream and lush meadow area with willows and wildflowers, including lupine, monkshood, Lewis monkeyflower, paintbrush, ranger's buttons and groundsel. You then ascend to an open area with aspen, sagebrush, and grasses that provides views of the volcanic ridgeline to your west. The next 0.5 mile or so is a pleasant, mostly level walk through wildflowers and scattered aspen groves quaking in the wind. Beautiful mountain views are available in every direction. You then begin a gentle ascent into a forest of scattered conifers, then downhill again past a luscious meadow with more mountain views before you reach the Pacific Crest Trail at 4.9 miles in from your trailhead. Across the large open meadow, you will see a charming old cowboy cabin, once the summer grazing home of the Meiss family, whom the meadows are named after.

You have now reached the Pacific Crest Trail (PCT), which travels from Canada to Mexico. If Mexico is your goal, turn left, and in a few months you will be there on the PCT. If you would prefer heading up to Canada, turn right. Either way, it's a long trip. This junction is located at the southernmost point of the Tahoe Rim Trail, and as you turn right at the junction you begin heading north. For about the next 50 miles the PCT and TRT are one trail. In addition to the Pacific Crest Trail and the Tahoe Rim

Trail, your footpath is now also a part of the Tahoe-Yosemite Trail (TYT), which travels from Tuolumne Meadows in Yosemite to Meeks Bay on the west shore of Lake Tahoe, a distance of a little over 185 miles. The PCT/TRT and TYT are one trail for the next 29 miles, until the TYT heads over Phipps Pass, past a chain of lakes known as the Tallant Lakes, down to Meeks Bay.

You turn right at this junction and begin your journey northwest with a lovely walk up the long valley of the Upper Truckee River. With high volcanic ridges to the east and west, and a beautiful almost-level valley floor to walk across, seasonally filled with wildflowers, it can be a highlight of your day. The flowers will vary from year to year, but you can expect to see low lying lupine and elephant heads in prolific display. As you walk northwest for about 0.5 mile on the PCT, Meiss Lake can be seen across 0.5 mile of swampy meadow to the north. This very shallow, warm lake makes a pleasant swimming hole in late summer. During the early summer, the walk to the lake is swampy, and you may lose blood to mosquitoes.

Mostly through the meadow you meet the Upper Truckee River, a good source for water or for catching your breath, but a potentially wet ford in early summer. After 1.5 miles through the meadow, a fairly steep climb awaits you for the last 0.5 mile up to Showers Lake. This steady uphill push through a mixture of deep forest and open fields gives you prolific displays of tall lupine, fireweed and paintbrush. As you rise, you will be rewarded with glorious views to the south and east of Meiss Meadows and the Dardanelles.

Showers Lake itself is beautiful (although often crowded with campers). The south side is marshy but the northern side provides great swimming opportunities enhanced by flat granite rocks that reach down to the water. Several camping spots surrounded by hemlock, lodgepole pines, and before late summer, mosquitoes, can be found above the north and east sides of the lake. To continue past Showers Lake, your trail first heads steeply down below the lake's outlet, and then climbs back up on the other side of the

Meiss Meadows

outlet's gully. You head for the next 0.5 mile through a pleasant forest with scattered trees and a few wildflower-dotted meadows until reaching the edge of an enormous bowl. This 0.7-mile-wide bowl is a beautiful mixture of castle-shaped volcanic rock formations, little streams plunging down steep rocky gullies, thick fields of lupine and paintbrush, and sometimes even late season snowfields. Several swiftly moving cascades, and stunning views to the east of Lake Tahoe, Dardanelles Lake, and Freel Peak complete this idyllic picture. It is a gentle climb across the bowl and during mid-summer the streams cascading down from the slopes above provide water for you and support an abundance of wildflowers. Near the end of the bowl, the path becomes steeper and the terrain, drier, until you reach a minor saddle on a crest where the surroundings change. Now you enter an area with sandy soils and scattered trees; mostly western white pine, lodgepole pine and hemlock. First you climb slowly, and then the trail levels off and soon reaches the Schneider Cow Camp Trail, which turns to your left and heads first west and then southwest. Now at 1.9 miles north of Showers Lake you continue north and make a 0.2-mile moderate descent to a saddle with an unmarked trail. Past this saddle junction your broad-crest trail continues through the open hemlock forest, making several minor ascents and descents before leveling off and passing several more small meadows. At 3.5 miles from Showers Lake (and 1.6 miles north of the Schneider Cow Camp trail junction), you meet another saddle junction, where a faded marked trail leads to Sayles Canyon. The Trail appears to be in danger of disappearing altogether.

The TRT continues along the sandy crest, mostly devoid of views, until a nice view opens up to the northwest, of Pyramid Peak, the tallest peak of the huge granite ridgeline known as the Crystal Range, which lies in the heart of Desolation Wilderness. Tahoe Rim Trail thru-hikers will get much closer views of the Crystal Range as they walk along Lake Aloha about 15 miles north of here, but first you must finish this section. At 4.4 miles from Showers Lake, you reach Bryan Meadow, and the Bryan Meadow Trail, which is about 3.9 miles from the Echo Summit trailhead. (See sidetrip "Bryan Meadow Trail.")

On the TRT just past the meadow you first descend briefly east to a minor gully, then climb, sometimes steeply, through a thick forest almost 0.5 mile to a ridge. After a steep uphill, what do you do next? Go downhill steeply of course, passing a rock outcropping just off the trail to the right. From here views can be enjoyed of the Upper Truckee River Canyon, South Lake Tahoe Airport and Lake Tahoe in the distance. Your trail quickly levels off and you pass a pleasant little camping spot next to a small, usually reliable, stream in a flat area in the trees. This is one of the last good spots to camp before you reach Echo Summit.

SIDETRIP Bryan Meadow Trail

The Bryan Meadow Trail will join the Sayles Canyon Trail, and as one, it descends an additional 0.6 miles to reach trailhead parking near the Sierra-at-Tahoe ski area. These trails provide another means to access Showers Lake for those in the Upper Highway 50 area. Bryan Meadow is a large, gently sloping meadow of grass and seasonal mud, but with no apparent drinking water near the trail. However, you should find water about 0.5 mile down the Sayles Canyon trail, at or just below the west end of the meadow.

Beyond it you begin a descent that starts out steep, and becomes really steep as the trail heads down along the side of a granite ridge. The last time I walked this trail I described this downhill as bone-jarring, toe-jamming, and knee-breaking. And those are just the words I can repeat. Since the first edition of this book the TRTA has added several switchbacks easing the grade, but it is still very steep. The rocky descent is so steep at times, it becomes slippery, so watch your step. The trail follows the east ridge of a big granite canyon that ends at Benwood Meadow. Take a few foot breaks to enjoy the beautiful granite rock formations and the especially large hemlocks you pass. Keep your eyes open for marmots as this is their prime territory. Gazing across this deep canyon, you see a higher ridge of granite on the west side. You pass a massive juniper at a crest saddle, which provides a viewpoint to the south. Views are highlighted by the Dardanelles and Round Top peak, which holds its north-facing snow fields well into late summer. Eventually the downhill largely abates, after a grueling 2-mile descent, where you cross the canyon's stream on a wooden bridge, and head into a lush shady area loaded with tiger lilies, thimbleberries, and ferns. Over the next 0.75 mile you continue on a gentle downhill, with Benwood Meadow visible through the trees on your right. By the meadow's northeast edge, you reach a junction with an older trail coming from a little-used alternate trailhead. With only 0.75 mile remaining, turn left at the junction and ascend gently north through a more open, drier forest of large Jeffrey pines and manzanita. A short distance before reaching the parking area you cross an old dirt road on a mostly treeless slope, formerly a ski area, and head past the headquarters of the California Conservation Corps on your right. Walk next to a parking lot to your car or Highway 50 and the next stretch of the Tahoe Rim Trail.

Echo Summit/Echo Lake to Barker Pass

(32.5 miles from Echo Lake, 34.7 miles from Echo Summit)

Difficulty—This strenuous section has many ascents and descents. While other segments of the Rim Trail can be hiked or biked in a day, this trip for most requires at least two days, and I recommend three. It can also be completed in sections by hiking out to Fallen Leaf Lake on the Glen Alpine trail, or to Emerald Bay from either Dicks Lake or Middle Velma Lake via the Bay View Trail.

Best Seasons—In the typical year, most of this section is snow free from mid-July to late October. Sections of this trail, especially the area on the north side of Dicks Pass, may have patches of snow into August following heavy snow years.

Highlights—A wonderful wilderness experience awaits you as you travel through the heart of Desolation Wilderness. There are many beautiful lakes, that you will pass by or see from the trail, including Lower Echo, Upper Echo, Cagwin, Ralston, Tamarack, Aloha, Heather, Susie, Grass, Gilmore, Half Moon, Alta Morris, Dicks, Fontanillis, Upper Velma, Middle Velma, and Richardson. If you like to swim in mountain lakes, this is the trail for you. You will also cross a high mountain pass with incredible views into two enormous watersheds.

Heads Up!—The starting elevation is about 7400 feet at Echo Lake, and you will rise to nearly 9400 feet at Dicks Pass. Water is plentiful for most of the trail, until you get north of Middle Velma Lake where the water supplies can quickly decline between it and Richardson Lake. Beyond the latter, there are several streams and springs. The biggest year-round stream along this stretch is Miller Creek, located about 1.75 miles north of Richardson Lake. A few miles farther gets you to Bear Creek. If you are thru-hiking, con-

Dicks Pass above Dicks Lake

sider that north of Barker Pass it is another 2 miles before you reach water again.

Wilderness permits are required to enter Desolation Wilderness. Day-use permits are available at the trailhead. If you are camping you must obtain a permit through the Forest Service. (Permit information can be found in Chapter 1.) The biggest concern with this section of trail, however, is that it is so magnificent you may want to stay forever, so be sure to bring along enough food.

Getting There, Echo to Barker—This trail begins at either Echo Summit or Lower Echo Lake. Most people prefer to start at Lower Echo Lake, where you can avoid 2.2 miles of mostly viewless hiking, much of it close to Highway 50 or amongst summer cabins.

Getting There, Echo Summit to Lower Echo Lake—From Meyers take Highway 50 westbound to Echo Summit. From the summit, drive just 0.3 mile and turn left. You will see an Echo Summit Sno-Park sign and then a California Conservation Corps

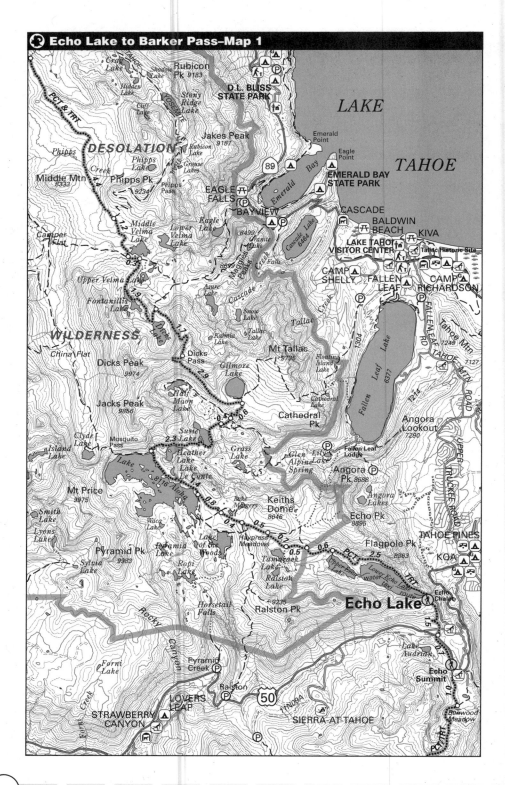

LAKE

TAHOE

D.L. BLISS
STATE PARK

Rubicon
Pk 9183

Craig
Lake

Shadow
Lake

Hidden
Lake

Stony
Ridge
Lake

Cliff
Lake

PCT & TRT

YOSEMITE

Jakes Peak
9187

Emerald
Point

Eagle
Point

DESOLATION

Rubicon
Lake

Jakes Peak
9187

Phipps

Phipps
Lake

Grouse
Lakes

EMERALD BAY
STATE PARK

Middle Mtn
8333

Phipps Pk
9234

Phipps
Pass

EAGLE
FALLS

Emerald
Bay

CASCADE

BALDWIN
BEACH

KIVA

Camper
Flat

Middle
Velma
Lake

Lower
Velma
Lake

Eagle
Lake

8499

Granite
Lake

BAYVIEW

Cascade Lake
6464

LAKE TAHOE
VISITOR CENTER

Tallac Historic Site

Upper Velma Lake

Azure
Lake

8899

Magnus
Peak

Cascade
Creek

Cascade

Falls

CAMP
SHELLY

FALLEN
LEAF

CAMP
RICHARDSON

Fontanillis
Lake

7.9

Snow
Lake

Tallac

Creek

1304

Tahoe Mtn
7249

WILDERNESS

China Flat

Dicks
Pass

Kalmia
Lake

Tallac
Lake

Mt Tallac
9735

Floating
Island
Lake

Fallen
Leaf
Lake
6377

7127

Dicks Peak
9974

2.9

Gilmore
Lake

Cathedral
Lake

1244

Angora
Lookout
7290

Jacks Peak
9856

Half
Moon
Lake

0.4 0.8

Cathedral
Pk

Clyde
Lake

Mosquito
Pass

Susie
Lake

2.3

Grass
Lake

Glen
Alpine
Spring

Lily
Lake

Fallen Leaf
Lodge

Island
Lake

Lake

Heather
Lake
Le Conte

.8 .16 along

1.4

Angora
Pk 8588

Angora
Lakes

Mt Price
9975

0.8

Lake
Margery

Keiths
Dome
8646

Echo Pk
8895

Smith
Lake

Waca
Lake

0.4

TAHOE PINES

Lyons
Lake

Lake
of the
Woods

Haypress
Meadows

0.5

0.7

0.6

Flagpole Pk
8363

KOA

Pyramid Pk
9983

Pyramid
Lake

Ropi
Lake

0.5

PCT

2.5

Sylvia
Lake

Tamarack
Lake

Upper Echo

Lower Echo
water taxi
route

TRT

Echo
Chalet

Rocky

Canyon

Horsetail
Falls

Ralston
Lake

9235

Ralston Pk

Echo Lake

1.5

Lake
Audrian

Forni
Creek

Pyramid
Creek

Ralston

50

11N09A

Echo
Summit

0.1

Benwood
Meadow

LOVERS
LEAP

STRAWBERRY
CANYON

SIERRA-AT-TAHOE

PCT TRT

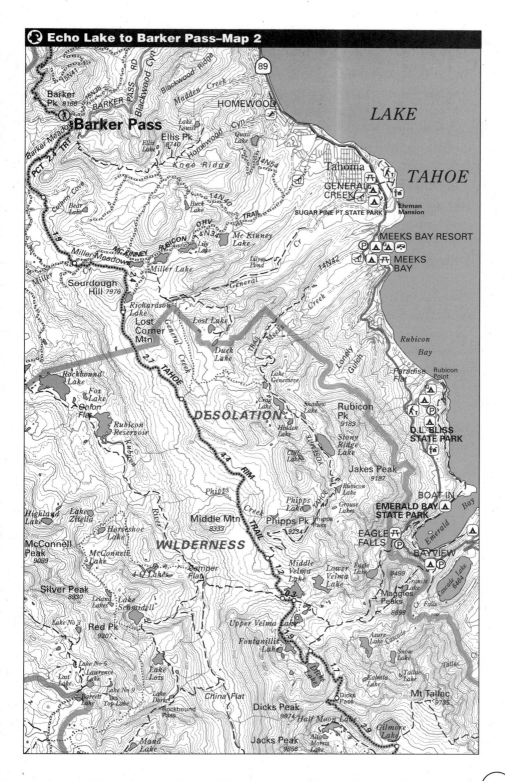

sign. Park in the parking lot and then walk to the western edge of the lot where you will see a Pacific Crest Trail/Tahoe Rim Trail sign marker. The trail parallels Highway 50 west through a mostly level to gently downhill, lightly forested area with some large red fir, western white pine, and lodgepole pine. You meet a dirt road 0.7 mile from the start; cross the road and turn right, then cross above a creek to adjacent Highway 50. Cross this very busy highway to where the trail resumes on the other side. Now the trail heads uphill through a thicker forest for 0.2 mile to Johnson Pass Road, the access road that you would take if you were starting at Echo Lake. You cross the road and head up a steep embankment and see a swift moving stream to the left. With 1.1 miles to go to Lower Echo Lake, the trail crosses the stream, which could be challenging when filled with mid-summer snowmelt. Walk through a lush and moist forest that will hold the snow until mid-summer, and then provide late summer wildflowers. Soon after, you pass several summer cabins and head downhill to the Lower Echo Lake's parking area. Cross this large paved parking lot, and another smaller dirt parking lot, to a short trail. You will find restroom facilities and the Echo Chalet Store here before you cross the lake's dam and reach the main trailhead.

Getting There, from Lower Echo Lake—From South Lake Tahoe drive west on Highway 50 to Echo Summit. From Echo Summit, drive 1 mile and turn right on Johnson Pass Road. Take this road 0.6 mile to a junction, where you will turn left on Echo Lakes Road. Go an additional 0.9 mile to a large parking lot above the lake. The resort requests that people using the trail not park in the lower parking lot near the lake. You reach the trail by walking from the Echo Chalet Store, and the lower parking lot, over the dam to a Tahoe Rim Trail sign. This section of the Tahoe Rim Trail is also part of the Tahoe-Yosemite Trail and the Pacific Crest Trail. It is one of the more popular trails into Desolation Wilderness.

Getting There, Barker Pass to Echo Lake/Summit—Take

Susie Lake and Crystal Range

Highway 89 (West Lake Blvd.) about 4.25 miles south from Tahoe City and turn right onto Blackwood Canyon Road, starting opposite Kaspian Beach. Drive 7 miles to the crest above Blackwood Canyon to where the paved road turns to dirt, then another 0.2 mile to the Pacific Crest Trail trailhead dirt parking lot on your right. To access the trail, walk south across the dirt road and walk uphill about 50 yards.

Barker Pass Road is closed during the winter months. The road has a gate at the entrance and another one 2.5 miles farther, just above the road's crossing of Blackwood Creek. The road is not plowed and these gates stay closed until the snow is melted to the top of Barker Pass. If you are planning on using the Barker Pass trailhead before mid-July, be sure and contact the TRTA to make sure that Barker Pass Road is open. Drive carefully on this narrow road, as it is popular for bike riding.

Trail Description

From Lower Echo Lake's dam, the trail heads initially east and uphill, and near a switchback west you can have a view toward South Lake Tahoe and Meyers. Especially prominent from the view is the Angora Fire of 2007, which came within a few miles of reaching Echo Lake (and a solid band of granite). You walk west above the northern shore of the long narrow Lower Echo Lake. Your route is mostly minor ups and downs, bordered by spectacular granite formations and the deep blue lake and surrounding mountains. The most dramatic granite cliff towering above you to the north is topped with a flagpole, which explains why its name is Flagpole Peak (8363 feet). The trail rambles for about 1 mile and passes a few gnarled junipers and Jeffrey pines that are hanging on through cracks in the granite. Then it ascends above lakeshore cabins. Your footing becomes more challenging as the terrain becomes rockier. You pass the west end of Lower Echo Lake. Magnificent views of the entire lake open up and you will see some more charming rustic cabins along its granite shore. If you yell at Echo Lakes on a nice calm day, you are supposed to get an echo back.

After a traverse, you then curve south over the rocky peninsula between Lower and Upper Echo Lakes. At 2.5 miles you come to a junction. A left turn takes you on a short trail down to a pier, which provides access to Upper Echo Lake and the Echo Lakes Water Taxi. The resort provides this fee service for homeowners who reside along the lakes, and for hikers heading into Desolation Wilderness. The water taxi, which travels from the Echo Chalet and marina at the east end of Lower Echo Lake to Upper Echo Lake, cuts off 2.5 miles from your hiking distances (5 miles round trip). For information on the Water Taxi call the Echo Chalet at (530) 659-7207. The taxi pier is also a great location for an afternoon swim.

Continue on the TRT from the junction, and climb steadily on more rocky terrain. You can enjoy breathtaking views of both Upper and Lower Echo lakes from this section of trail. Upper Echo Lake is especially striking with its multiple granite islands topped with windblown trees. At 0.6 mile from the boat taxi your trail levels off briefly and you arrive at the boundary of Desolation Wilderness. To hike beyond this point requires a permit, which should be obtained at the trailhead or through the Forest Service (permit information is found in Chapter 1). You will be hiking in Desolation Wilderness for more than 20 miles on the Tahoe Rim Trail. Just past the wilderness boundary you reach a junction. To your right, there is a trail that leads steeply uphill to Triangle Lake, with access to Echo Peak (8895 feet). (See sidetrip "Triangle Lake.")

You continue on the TRT/PCT, climbing 0.5 mile to a junction on your left that leads to nearby Tamarack Lake. The trail to this charming lake is located 3.6 miles from the Echo Lakes

> ### SIDETRIP **Triangle Lake**
>
> This side trail leads to Triangle Lake, then over a steep ridge down to just east of Lily Lake and then by road down to Fallen Leaf Lake. The steep downhill trip is pretty with many lush stream crossings loaded with early summer wildflowers. The trail faces north, however, with snow lasting well into the summer. If you hike this section before July you may find several dangerous icy spots.

Trailhead (and just 1.1 miles from the taxi), just inside the wilderness boundary. While it is a great place to stop, its proximity to the trailhead means it will be very busy. Your views are glorious with the imposing Ralston Peak (9235 feet) to the south, and Echo Peak to the northeast.

After another 0.7 mile of rocky climbing, you reach another junction on your right, also leading toward Fallen Leaf Lake.

The climb west finally abates in 0.4 mile at a junction in Haypress Meadows. Here you encounter a mixed forest of red firs, mountain hemlocks, and western white pines scattered around small grassy meadows that bloom with wildflowers throughout the spring and summer. The trail southwest heads over to Lake of the Woods, as does a southbound one 300 yards later. About 150 yards past it you meet a trail descending north to lovely Lake Lucille and Lake Margery. About 0.3 mile later, at 5.2 miles from your trailhead, you meet another junction. The left turn takes you 0.5 mile west down to the southeast corner of Lake Aloha (from where one can wind 0.75 mile west over to the lake's 20-foot-high dam just above granite-lined America Lake). The TRT and PCT go straight ahead, through an area thick with midsummer wildflowers, to the east shore of Lake Aloha in 0.8 mile. This heavily forested trail section may be covered in snow through early summer.

Lake Aloha (8116 feet) provides an incredible, unique landscape. There are only a few wind-beaten trees surrounding the lake, with hundreds of small flat rock islands scattered across its surface. The Crystal Range, a huge ridge of granite, topped by pointy Pyramid Peak (9983 feet) in the south, and Mt. Price (9976 feet) in the north, rises right up from the western shores of the lake. The trail meanders between granite boulders hugging the shore of Lake Aloha. Above the lake to the east is Cracked Crag, a big pile of rocks that families of marmots call home. Along the entire length of the barren landscape above Lake Aloha, you will find great swimming and camping spots. Aloha is one of my favorite places to take children camping. The little islands are fun to swim to and the expanses of flat granite are perfect to lie on and gaze at Pyramid Peak. A dam controls the waters of Lake Aloha and the lake's size decreases dramatically in the fall. That great waterside spot you visited in June may be a long distance from the shore after Labor Day.

When you reach the northeast corner of the lake, you meet a junction, 1.4 miles from the last. Straight ahead a trail goes over Mosquito Pass (sounds enticing doesn't it? It's actually quite nice and leads to lots of great lakes and camping spots). The TRT turns right, following the sign, which says Glen Alpine. With Freel Peak (10,881 feet) visible in the distance the trail begins a descent, that in 0.5 mile will bring you to the north shore of Heather Lake. Along the way, you will pass stunning multi-colored rocky panoramas, lots of flowing water, early summer wildflowers, hemlock, and mountain heather topped with its small red flowers. In the early summer much of this area may be under snow. Heather Lake is a picturesque large mountain lake with several tree-topped islands. A limited supply of campsites can be found above the lake. Your 0.3-mile traverse along the north side of the lake toward its

Heather Lake and the Crystal Range

outlet provides a special photo opportunity looking west: Heather Lake's biggest island is in the foreground, and the Crystal Range looms above the lake in the background.

Just past Heather Lake, a very unique phenomenon is often visible in spring or early summer. Where the outlet creek melts under the snow, it forms a snow tunnel. I have seen it where the entrance to the snowcave was 10 feet high and at least 30 feet deep. Stepping into the cave will provide you with a shower as well as the sight of the sun filtering through the blue geodesic shapes of the suncups above.

You now walk over a low, rocky saddle and begin a short descent to Susie Lake, another beautiful Sierra lake, and this one bordered by red rock and dotted with islands. Susie Lake is loaded with campsites near its shore, many of which are illegal. Camps are required to be at least 200 feet from the shores of any lake, and you may be cited if you camp any nearer to the water. Unfortunately, Susie Lake can be quite busy due to its short distance of about 4 miles from the popular Glen Alpine trailhead above Fallen Leaf Lake. The trail circles about half of the lake and offers views of the very imposing Dicks Peak (9974 feet) to the northwest, Jacks

Peak (9856 feet) to the west and the saddle of Dicks Pass (north) 1600 feet above you. This awesome view may lose some of its appeal when you realize that Dicks Pass is your next major goal.

Consider stopping at Susie Lake to relax and swim before making the big jaunt up the hill (and Susie can be quite warm by mid-summer). About halfway along your trip around the lake, just before you reach the outlet for Susie Lake, about 1 mile past Heather Lake's outlet and a little over 9 miles from your trailhead, go around the bend to the right and traverse along the side of the hill about 50 yards to a tremendous viewpoint of Grass Lake and Keiths Dome to the southeast. Then, return to the trail and cross the outlet creek. In the spring this crossing can be quite a challenge. Try going slightly upstream and cross on the logs. Be careful. Across the creek, hopefully still dry, continue around Susie Lake on the rocky terrain. After 0.25 mile, the trail veers east away from the lake and heads downhill (yes downhill, all of which and more must be made up a little farther on). In about 0.5 mile you reach a junction. A right turn heads 3.8 miles to the Glen Alpine trailhead above Fallen Leaf Lake. You, however will continue straight ahead on the TRT. After a short distance of 0.4 mile, you meet another junction that will take you to Half Moon Lake. (See sidetrip "Half Moon Lake.")

A right leads you to Fallen Leaf Lake in 3.6 miles. From here, the TRT begins a climb of 3.5 miles to Dicks Pass at 9380 feet. After a steady uphill grind, climbing dozens of wide steps, you reach a junction at 0.6 mile from the Half Moon Lake trail junction. To visit Gilmore Lake, you can go an additional 0.2 mile straight ahead from the Dicks Pass/Gilmore Lake junction. Gilmore Lake is a large round lake bordered by big red firs and lodgepole pines that

SIDETRIP **Half Moon Lake**

Turning left at the junction just beyond the Glen Alpine trailhead junction, you will be headed toward Half Moon Lake, which you will reach in just 1.2 miles. Alta Morris Lake is an additional 0.7 mile. These lakes are both worthwhile goals for another trip. They lie at the foot of Dicks Peak and Jacks Peak, at the edge of a massive cirque. They may be less crowded than lakes along the TRT/PCT.

Middle Velma Lake

makes a pleasant spot for a visit, or an overnight stay, especially if you want to hike up nearby Mt. Tallac (9735 feet), which is about 1.75 miles farther and about 1450 feet higher. Tallac's panoramic views of Lake Tahoe are considered among the best. At just under 11 miles from the Echo Lake trailhead, Gilmore might make an excellent camping choice.

Ahead the TRT is well graded. Starting gently, it then becomes a more moderate climb toward a conspicuous saddle. Along the way, the views of Susie Lake, Half Moon Lake and Alta Morris Lake are magnificent. In the summer, and sometimes as late as early fall, wildflowers grow in abundance here, especially paintbrush and lupine, which may be seen in huge fields of flowers. In the fall you may also see an occasional explorer's gentian. While much of the journey is treeless, you will pass several gnarled junipers, which have been battered by the wind, as well as some hemlocks and western white pines. The trail reaches the saddle between Dicks Pass and Dicks Peak at 9974 feet elevation. From this location, your north view includes all of Dicks Lake directly below, as well as Fontanillis Lake, Middle Velma Lake, and a wide panorama of mountains in the distance including Twin Peaks (8878 feet) about

20 miles away, and on a clear day, Lassen Peak (10,457 feet) at over 130 miles away. Since the trail is covered in snow much of the year, it is important to understand the distinction between the saddle and the pass. While from the saddle it is another 200 feet of climbing to the pass, don't try to avoid the climb by starting toward Dicks Lake from the saddle. It is a very steep north-facing slope that is covered in ice for much of the year. To reach the pass, continue on the trail east past a few particularly twisted whitebark pines to a level, treeless pass at 9380 feet. You have now climbed 1100 feet over 2.9 miles, since the junction near Gilmore Lake. Once you reach the top of the pass, you may be ready to collapse, I mean relax, and enjoy the view. And what a view! To the south, you can see Lake Aloha, Pyramid Peak and the tip of Mt. Price, Susie Lake, Half Moon Lake, Alta Morris Lake, and all the way south-southeast to Round Top (10,381 feet) about 20 miles away. Towering above you to the west is the very imposing Dicks Peak and, to the southeast, Jacks Peak, both bearing patches of snow that will last throughout most of the year. The best viewpoint is actually just before the top of the pass on a flat rock to the south of the trail.

You've had your fun. Now 13.6 miles into your route, it is time for the long downhill to Dicks Lake. In the next 1.7 miles you drop about 900 feet via a number of switchbacks to a saddle above Dicks Lake. While the south-facing side of Dicks Pass is loaded with grasses and wildflowers growing in the volcanic soil and between the rocks, the north-facing side of fractured granite is dominated by thick stands of mountain hemlock with just a few grasses here and there. A north-facing slope near 9000 feet elevation on the western side of the Sierra holds a tremendous amount of snow for much of the year. Thus the growing season is too short for most trees except the hardy hemlock. In addition, the hemlock is so prolific that it shades out the competition. At the saddle east of and above Dicks Lake you meet a junction. (See sidetrip "Emerald Bay.")

A left at the saddle continues your TRT/PCT journey. After a 0.2-mile descent southeast, you reach a short spur trail south to Dicks Lake, a large lake with plenty of space along its shore to roam or camp. Tucked away on the shady north side of Dicks Peak, this lake may still be frozen over in July after a big winter. At about 15.5 miles from your trailhead, with about 17 easier miles to go, this locale may be a good one to spend the night. From the

> **SIDETRIP Emerald Bay**
>
> A right turn at the junction east and above Dicks Lake will take you to Emerald Bay in 4.9 miles via the Bay View Trail. Straight ahead, northwest, is a rock knob. With a quick scramble, you will discover tremendous views here. Fontanillis Lake and Dicks Peak can be seen respectively to the west and south.

spur trail, your trail veers northwest and continues another 0.3 mile to Fontanillis Lake, one of my favorites. Exposed granite and a few scattered hardy trees surround Fontanillis Lake. The trail approaches the granite-lined lakeshore in about 0.3 mile, but takes another 0.3 mile to reach its shore. You hike in and out of numerous little bays, all with glorious views of Dicks Peak hulking above. Many great lunch and swimming spots are found along the way (perhaps a bit cold for a swim, but how about a quick jump in?). At the end of the lake, at 0.3 mile farther down, the trail crosses its outlet creek (another tough early season crossing) and descends toward Middle Velma Lake. (See sidetrip "Upper Velma Lake.")

> **SIDETRIP Upper Velma Lake**
>
> For another interesting sidetrip, follow the creek you crossed as it falls down a steep granite slab almost 0.5 mile to Upper Velma Lake. The granite slab is steep enough that the water, which is usually quite shallow, cascades down the slope, but it is not too steep to prevent you from walking right next to the water. A trail runs from Upper Velma Lake to Middle Velma Lake, where you can rejoin the Tahoe Rim Trail, or head out to Emerald Bay.

After crossing Fontanillis Lake's outlet creek, you begin a descent through a deep forest of mostly red firs. In 0.8 mile of walking, and about 400 feet of descent, you reach a junction where the TRT heads left (west). A right turn would lead you out to Emerald Bay, about 5 miles away. On the TRT in a short distance you see Middle Velma Lake, a large lake with many islands that makes for a great camping or swimming spot, although like much of Desolation Wilderness, it can be quite popular in the summer. If you are continuing north, be aware that the next lake, Richardson Lake, is smaller and marshier. Its accessibility by 4-wheel-drive vehicles makes it less attractive to those backpackers hoping to enjoy a motor-free experience.

Once you have relaxed or camped at Middle Velma Lake, 17.5 miles from the Echo Lakes trailhead, you continue your journey north along the TRT/PCT. This second half of the hike from the Velma Lakes to Barker Pass is dramatically different than the first half that began at Echo Lake. While the first half goes through the heart of Desolation Wilderness, with more rocks than trees and beautiful rock-lined lakes (and lots of people), you are now embarking on a 15-mile journey through forest with only one lake (and fewer people). Before you leave Middle Velma Lake, be sure to filter water: the next reliable source is Richardson Lake 8.3 miles north.

Shortly after you leave Middle Velma Lake, you meet a junction, 0.3 mile past the previous one. Here a trail heads west down to Camper Flat and provides access to a whole host of Desolation Wilderness lakes and the Rubicon River. From this intersection the TRT/PCT/TYT turns north and in 0.3 mile crosses boggy lands bordering Middle Velma Lake's outlet creek. It then goes 0.9 mile gently uphill to a junction with the Phipps Pass Trail, which turns off to the right. (See sidetrip "Meeks Bay.")

The TRT/PCT continues for the next 4.4 miles after the junction with the Phipps Pass Trail to a junction with a faint trail, which heads over to Lake Genevieve. (This little-used trail is overgrown in many spots and is not recom-

SIDETRIP **Meeks Bay**

At this point, the Tahoe-Yosemite Trail parts company with the PCT/TRT. The Phipps Pass Trail would lead you about 12 miles to Meeks Bay (and the terminus of the TYT). Along the way, you pass Phipps Peak (9234 feet) and Rubicon, Stony Ridge, Shadow, Crag and Genevieve lakes. If you have been hiking all the way from Yosemite you are almost home. A wonderful point-to-point hike starts at Emerald Bay and ends at Meeks Bay via the Velma Lakes and Phipps Pass. This 18-mile route takes you by a string of lakes and exceptional viewpoints.

mended.) There are two important features along this 4.4-mile stretch. The first is seasonal Phipps Creek, reached after a 1.5-mile, mostly gentle descent. You could camp near it. The second is after a 2-mile, erratic ascent to a high point with a short spur trail west, from which you can survey the Rubicon River lands. Past this you descend 0.9 mile to the next trail junction. You pass several small meadows blooming with asters, Queen Anne's lace, groundsel, corn lilies and elephant heads. Thru-hikers are the primary users of this lightly used section of trail. If you meet someone who is hiking all the way from Mexico to Canada, be sure to take advantage of the opportunity and talk to them about their experiences. They have already walked over 1,100 miles and surely have some fascinating stories to tell. One thing is certain, if they have made it this far, they are persistent.

Beyond the junction with the trail to Lake Genevieve, the combined PCT/TRT begins by going downhill. You can enjoy the views of Mt. Tallac and Dicks Peak in the distance to the south. As the trail moves into a more densely forested area, you will be leaving Desolation Wilderness at its north boundary, about 1.5 miles past the junction. Then 0.75 mile north of the wilderness, traversing along the base of Lost Corner Mountain, you reach a minor saddle. Next, you head 0.7 mile down to the northwest corner of tree-lined Richardson Lake. This pleasant little lake has several nice campsites set among the trees, but look out for mosquitoes in the spring. Richardson Lake, about 6.7 miles from the Barker Pass trailhead, is accessible via a 4-wheel-drive dirt road so be prepared for outdoor recreational vehicles, the main users of the north-shore campsites.

From Richardson Lake, the trail heads north, first descending the lower east slopes of Sourdough Hill, then proceeding west above Miller Meadows, beyond which it crosses two dirt roads. Just past the first road (about 2 miles from Richardson Lake) you cross Miller Creek, a good source of water and a potentially difficult creek to cross in the spring. The second road crossing, about 200 yards farther, is the very popular McKinney Rubicon OHV

Trail, which heads east down to the McKinney Estates subdivision on the west shore of Lake Tahoe, or west on a famously difficult stretch of 4-wheel terrain to the Rubicon River.

Onward, your journey is pleasant as you pass through thick fir forest and occasional small meadows opulent with wildflowers. The gently rolling terrain heads northwest 1.5 miles to Bear Lake's sparkling outlet creek, then 0.4 farther up to the Bear Lake Road.

Turn left on the road, walk about 50 yards to trail, and stay just above the road. You now have a 2 mile, 420-foot ascent to Forest Route 3. On it you will first pass one good sized stream and then several smaller ones. Most promote wildflowers until late summer. The trail climbs through Barker Meadows with several open slopes dotted with mule ears and views of Barker Peak, as well as the first sunshine in many miles of deep forest. Eventually you reach Barker Pass where the trail ends on a major dirt road, which provides access through Blackwood Canyon to Lake Tahoe. The PCT/TRT from Barker Pass to Tahoe City begins across the road and slightly to the west.

SECTION 8

Barker Pass to Tahoe City

(16.7 miles)

Difficulty—This moderate to strenuous section has several good-sized climbs, but more of the trail runs downhill than uphill. The starting elevation is 7650 feet and it ends near the Truckee River at about 6300 feet. If you are starting from the Tahoe City end, it is more strenuous.

Best Seasons—This section can usually be hiked from late-July to mid-October (or until the first major snow). Most of the first 7 miles of this trail section are at high elevations that receive a lot of snow. Much of the trail faces north or east—a combination that leads to a late snow melt.

Highlights—There are beautiful ridgeline views of Lake Tahoe, Granite Chief Wilderness, both Blackwood and Ward canyons, and lush areas loaded with wildflowers in both canyons. Twin Peaks (8878 feet), a Sierra crest landmark, is accessible from the trail. In addition, there are numerous little stream crossings and several good camping spots. A lovely little waterfall cascades near one part of the trail in upper Ward Canyon. There is a very pretty series of meadows known as Page Meadows. A dense forest area with huge pines and firs grows in the Ward Creek watershed. Wildlife is abundant and includes bear, coyote, raccoon, blue grouse, and perhaps goshawk and spotted owls. Between Barker Pass and Twin Peaks this lakeless stretch tends to get less use than the trails in the Desolation Wilderness area, which has mountain lakes. However, in the Page Meadows vicinity, bikers, hikers and joggers abound. At the end of your trip you may find the Truckee River is a perfect place to swim or to complete your day with a rafting trip down the Truckee.

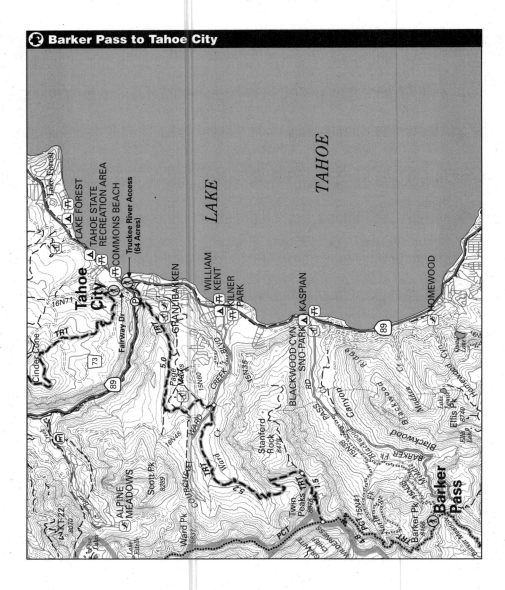

Heads Up!—In the fall, as streams dry up, the water supply can be limited. You reach the North Fork of Blackwood Creek, about 2.5 miles north of Barker Pass at the bottom of a meadow. In the next mile, you may find one or more springs before late summer. However, the most dependable water source is Ward Creek, about 8.5 miles north of Barker Pass. You parallel the creek, sometimes at a distance, for over 3 miles, and by the time you're starting north from the canyon's main road you have only 5 miles to the Tahoe City trailhead.

The only places to swim are the Truckee River at your destination, and at adjacent Lake Tahoe. The Commons public beach is about 0.25 mile east of the Tahoe Rim Trail on Highway 28 in the center of Tahoe City. There are lots of junctions and turnoffs on this section of trail and the Forest Service has been closing and rebuilding roads and trails in this area, so follow the TRT trail markers and pay attention to where you are going.

Barker Pass Road is not plowed and remains closed to cars until the snow melts in the spring or early summer. Often the road is not open until late June. The road is narrow in spots and is a favorite for bike riding. If you're a cyclist, observe the 20 mph speed limit and watch for rollerbladers, rollerskiers, wayward dogs, and moms with strollers.

Tips for Mountain Bikers—The first 5 miles of the TRT overlap with the PCT. As you know by now, bikes are not allowed on the PCT. From Twin Peaks to Tahoe City, bikes are allowed: Start at "64 Acres" in Tahoe City (also known as the Truckee River Access Parking Lot) and follow the TRT along the Truckee River, then head uphill rather steeply. In some places there are lots of loose rocks. After 1.7 miles, you reach the east edge of the Page Meadows area and a whole network of great biking trails. The TRT turns right at the first major junction (to the left, a trail crosses a small meadow and heads uphill into the trees), and provides a great gentle uphill ride through the forest above the perimeter of the meadows. In another 1.3 miles, you reach another junction, where you have two riding options:

Alternative Routes—Turn left and follow the TRT as it skirts the edge of a meadow and crosses another one. The section of trail is built-up 6 inches above the meadow to protect the fragile ecosystem. After passing Page Meadows, the trail heads into the woods. At first the TRT follows a moderate downhill course, then descends more steeply on an old dirt road. Just 0.25 mile before reaching Ward Creek Blvd., the TRT turns right, becomes a single track trail and heads southwest. From here you go more gently downhill, a short distance to Ward Creek Blvd., a major paved thoroughfare. The TRT continues directly across the road.

The alternative route to Ward Creek Boulevard and the TRT is to continue ahead for about 1 mile to the next major junction. Turn left and enjoy a fun downhill to Chamonix Road, a paved street in the Alpine Peaks subdivision. Take Chamonix downhill to Courchevel, turn left, and head downhill. In a little more than 1 mile, you will see the Tahoe Rim Trail on your right. (Along the way the road name changes from Courchevel to Ward Creek Boulevard.) From Ward Creek Blvd., the TRT follows an old dirt road for about 2 miles to a washed-out bridge. After the bridge, the trail starts uphill in earnest through a beautiful area of small meadows where aspens are interspersed with forests of tall old-growth trees. As the trail gets steeper, most bikers will walk their bikes or stop and turn around. Eventually, about 5.2 miles beyond Ward Creek Boulevard you reach a saddle between Twin Peaks on your right and Stanford Rock on the left. The trail to the right leads steeply uphill to Twin Peaks where bikes are not allowed. The trail to the left leads uphill very steeply to a great lookout point, and then a 4-mile fun downhill on a dirt road to Ward Creek Boulevard. Just before reaching the road, you cross Ward Creek in an area that can be deep and difficult to ford until late summer. The 4-mile section between Stanford Rock and Ward Creek is also a challenging but beautiful uphill ride. The start is about 0.5 mile

Twin Peaks from the head of Ward Canyon

east of the TRT on Ward Creek Road. You will see a gated trail leading off from the road next to a large open flat area on the south side of the highway. Immediately after passing the gate you will need to cross Ward Creek. The climb varies between moderately steep to very steep, and provides tremendous views of the lake and Blackwood Canyon. Eventually you reach the Stanford Rock viewpoint and a spectacular view of Ward Canyon, Twin Peaks and the Sierra crest. After enjoying the view, turn left and follow the trail downhill to a junction with the Tahoe Rim Trail. Or, you can turn around and ride back the way you came. If you choose to ride from here on the TRT, be prepared for a challenging and steep ride on loose soil, with several technical rocky sections.

Getting There, Barker Pass to Tahoe City—Take Highway 89 (West Lake Blvd.) about 4.25 miles south of Tahoe City and turn right onto the Blackwood Canyon Road, starting opposite Kaspian Beach. Drive 7 miles to the crest above Blackwood Canyon to where the paved road turns to dirt, then another 0.2 mile to the Pacific Crest Trail trailhead parking lot on your right; it is a dirt lot.

Getting There, Tahoe City to Barker Pass—From the intersection of Highway 89 and Highway 28 at the stoplight in Tahoe City, head south on Highway 89 0.25 mile to the Truckee River Access Parking Area (64 Acres). Park in the lot. The trail starts along the south side of the Truckee River. As you follow the Truckee River west and downstream the trail begins as a bike trail. Continue to follow the river downstream as the bike trail leads into a paved road that then becomes a dirt road. Walk on the dirt road for 0.3 mile and meet a gate right next to the Truckee River. Go around the gate and across a south-climbing gravel road to the start of the Tahoe Rim Trail.

Trail Description

At Barker Pass (7650 feet) the trail begins by traversing west around the south side of Barker Peak (8166 feet), where you get excellent views of Desolation Wilderness to the south. In 0.9 mile your moderately steep walk through a field of mule ears reaches the Sierra crest, where you will have views east down the expanse of Blackwood Canyon to Lake Tahoe. Beyond the crest, your route continues with a gentle ascent northeast across the canyon's upper slopes. In 0.25 mile you pass a beautiful stream bordered with aster, delphinium, tiger lily, columbine, paintbrush, and other wildflowers. After a pleasant walk gently up through mostly open volcanic terrain that is interrupted by a red fir forest, you cross a steep face to the base of two lofty volcanic plugs, about 0.5 mile past the stream. From here you have wide open views of Lake Tahoe and Blackwood Canyon to the east. From these lofty twin rock formations, the trail descends into a large bowl lush with wildflowers and greenery late into the summer. Mountain hemlock is now the dominant tree. These fascinating trees are laden with cones on their thick green foliage. The hemlock can be most easily identified by the drooping top of the tree, which gives it a fairy-tale appearance.

As you descend farther into this lovely bowl, you pass several

Volcanic plugs north of Barker Pass

areas graced by Sierra wildflowers including explorer's gentian, which blooms into the fall. At the bottom of the bowl, about 2.5 miles from the trailhead, is a great camping spot. It has a running stream (North Fork of Blackwood Creek), a nice flat place to rest your head, and views of Lake Tahoe and Blackwood Canyon. Just beyond this camping spot, the trail rounds a corner and continues to descend past several spring-fed creeks. It's a wildflower haven with late-season water and a continuing series of views. After about a 1-mile traverse from the camping spot, your trail starts a series of long switchbacks almost to the crest of the ridge. The climb begins in a dark viewless forest of large red fir trees. As you climb, you will see Ellis Peak to the southeast, Desolation Wilderness to the south, and almost all of Blackwood Canyon to the east. Just below the top of the crest, you round the ridge to find new views of the south side of Twin Peaks (8878 feet). Then you pass the Granite Chief Wilderness sign and quickly reach the Sierra crest, where there are views in all directions. To your north and west, you can see the full expanse of Granite Chief Wilderness, to the northeast, you see nearby Twin Peaks, to the east Lake Tahoe, and to the south Desolation Wilderness lies in the distance. In the foreground you can review the knife-edge ridge whose backside you just climbed.

Just 0.25 mile beyond this exposed viewpoint you meet a junction, at 4.8 miles from Barker Pass. This is where the Tahoe Rim Trail and Pacific Crest Trail part ways after running together for a total of about 50 miles. Straight ahead are the PCT and Canada. A right turn takes you along the southern slope of Twin Peaks on the Tahoe Rim Trail. Those of you without the time or inclination to hike to Canada, should turn right. In 0.5 mile you meet a spur trail to the top of the eastern Twin Peak. (For those hiking south, this is about 6.2 miles from the Ward Canyon trailhead.) If you are going to take this trail, be forewarned that it can be a bit treacherous, but the views are spectacular. A safer route is to head directly up to the saddle separating the two summits. From the summit trail junction, continue descending along a ridgeline on the TRT for 1 mile through a mixed forest of red fir, hemlock, and western white pine to a saddle. Along the route you will find scenic views of Squaw Valley and Alpine Meadows to the north. At the saddle you meet another junction. The Tahoe Rim Trail turns left, while the trail straight ahead would take you to Stanford Rock, as described in the mountain biking section.

You are now heading north down a rather steep hill through a deep forest of fir and hemlock trees into Ward Canyon. This portion of the trail is bone-jarringly steep with loose dark soil, but the views are glorious, especially of Twin Peaks to your left. After about 1.1 miles of downhill, you encounter a large meadow at the base of Twin Peaks. This beautiful meadow, surrounded with imposing peaks high above, is a splendid resting spot. Next, the descent is less steep and takes you into a more thinly forested section. You pass another meadow and then see 30-foot McCloud falls , just off the trail on your left. Switchback down toward Ward Creek for 0.9 mile, and then pass several lush meadows that are surrounded by aspen trees, as well as large red firs and Jeffrey pines. Cross Ward Creek at a recently constructed bridge. The usually

Twin Peaks and wind-whipped trees

swiftly moving creek is a great place to take a break and get your feet in the water before a few more dusty miles. Across the bridge you walk on a former road, which first traverses over 0.5 mile, and then heads gently downhill. After passing a washed-out bridge across a tributary of Ward Creek the trail joins an old dirt road. You can camp just past the bridge site, to the north of the road, in an opening in the trees, which was used as a Forest Service camp when they were building the Tahoe Rim Trail between here and Twin Peaks. You can usually find water in the creek, or in a spring on the northeast edge of the camp.

The TRT, which is now an old dirt road arching eastward, heads gently downslope for 1.75 miles through meadows and forest to a trailhead on Ward Creek Boulevard, a paved road leading up to Alpine Peaks, a development on the "backside" (south) of Alpine Meadows Ski Area. Along this stretch of trail, there are several nice views, including one of Grouse Rock, which you can see from a particularly pretty meadow that borders Ward Creek on your right. (Grouse Rock is the large volcanic rock on the ridgeline to the west between Twin Peaks and Ward Peak that sits right above the Pacific Crest Trail. It is a popular destination with backcountry skiers.) Your trail, blocked at the trailhead by a gate, was once used regularly as an off-highway vehicle route. In the New Year floods of 1997, the road was washed-out in several locations. Where it was once smooth dirt, the trail in many locations became a jumble of rocks where the soil washed away.

At Ward Creek Boulevard you see a Tahoe Rim Trail kiosk. With 5 miles to go to Tahoe City, cross the road and begin climbing on trail through a forest of white fir and Jeffrey pine. After about 0.25 mile the trail turns left onto a dirt road and heads uphill more steeply. Near the top of the hill, Ward Canyon, Ward Peak and the Sherwood Chairlift at Alpine Meadows Ski Area can be viewed through an opening in the trees. After a steep 0.6 mile, the trail levels at a junction with another dirt road. A right turn here would take you to eastern Page Meadows and the Talmont Estates development in about 1 mile. The TRT angles left and winds up through a young forest for 0.4 mile to the road's end, where posts were installed to block vehicles. Here a lateral trail heads left to the lowest of the Page Meadows and provides access to the Alpine Peaks neighborhood about 0.25 mile away. (See sidetrip "Oven.")

You are now in the Page Meadows area, a series of five interconnected meadows that serve as a popular retreat for hiking, mountain biking and cross-country skiing. The meadows provide an easily accessible outdoor haven for many residents who live in developments close by. They are especially popular as a place to go cross-country skiing on full moon nights.

From the lateral trail west the TRT goes straight ahead through the road gate and follows the meadow area on your left for a short

> **SIDETRIP Oven**
>
> Just off this lateral trail is an oven built by Basque sheepherders. Built in the 1950s, the oven provides evidence of a unique lifestyle once present in Page Meadows. Sit next to the oven and imagine sheepherders enjoying fresh baked bread while watching sheep graze in the meadow under the beautiful aspen trees.

distance before entering a large meadow. The trail is built up 6 inches above the meadow to prevent damage to this fragile ecosystem. About a third of the way across this beautiful meadow, you meet a trail starting east. This provides access to three other large meadows, as well as a route to Tahoe City. The TRT continues straight. At the end of the meadow, turn around to enjoy a tree-framed view of Twin Peaks. Your trail now heads north out of the meadow, into a grove of aspens before entering a forest of fir trees. About 0.2 mile from the meadow you meet another junction. (See sidetrip "Alpine Meadows.")

The TRT turns right (east), however, and parallels the mostly unseen meadows on your right. The next 1.3 miles are primarily downhill, with several short uphills. This is a very popular mountain biking section for good reason. It rolls along with lots of fun little twists and turns on a fairly smooth surface. The trail levels near the edge of a small meadow and you meet another junction. (See sidetrip "Raw hide Drive.")

The TRT turns left (east) and begins a 0.6-mile steep descent down a narrow canyon, with rocky and challenging (for bikes) terrain, to a junction. The Tahoe Rim Trail veers left. If you are on your bike and would like to avoid this difficult section, refer to the sidetrip above for an easier route to Tahoe City. From the TRT marker you travel almost 1 mile,

SIDETRIP Alpine Meadows

At the junction just mentioned, a spur trail leads left (west). In about 2 miles you would reach the Alpine Meadows residential area. In addition, spurs from this trail lead to the top of Scott Peak, the Alpine Meadows Ski Area, or Tahoe City via the bike trail along the Truckee River. These trails are fun mountain biking routes or pleasant hikes through the forest.

SIDETRIP Rawhide Drive

The right turn leads across a snippet of meadow and then after a short uphill, it runs into a major trail. Turn left and in 1.5 downhill miles, you reach Rawhide Drive, close to Tahoe City. If you want to head toward Tahoe City at this point, follow Rawhide north to Granlibakken Road, turn right here and follow Granlibakken Road to West Lake Boulevard, also known as Highway 89. Turn left on the bike trail and in 0.5 mile you will be in Tahoe City. A right-hand turn on this trail junction will take you to the biggest meadow in the Page Meadows area in 0.5 mile.

generally downhill, winding through the shade of the fir and sugar pine trees until you arrive at a trail junction on the Truckee River. Turn right and follow the trail 0.1 mile east to a gravel road where the trail tread ends. You now walk across the road and past a gate. Stop here to swim in the Truckee River or to watch summer rafters. Your trail is now a dirt road heading along the river upstream 0.3 mile to a paved road. The National Forest 64 Acres (Truckee River Access) parking lot is straight ahead.

From the parking lot, a 0.3-mile walk along bike paths and roads reaches the beginning of the next section of the Tahoe Rim Trail, from Tahoe City to Brockway Summit. Follow the bike trail to the pedestrian bridge across the Truckee River to Highway 89. Turn right, and follow the bike trail 50 yards to its end. Cross Highway 89 to Fairway Drive, which is directly across the highway. Go 0.2 mile up Fairway Drive to the Fairway Community Center parking lot on your right. The Tahoe Rim Trail continues across the street.

7

Other Tahoe Area Attractions and Activities

Once you have exhausted all of the recreation possibilities on the Tahoe Rim Trail, you may want to check out some other Tahoe area trails. Brief summaries of a few of my favorites are presented below.

Hiking

Emerald Bay

Difficulty—Easy. Depending on where you go, it is anywhere from 2 to 9 miles.

Map—Tahoe Rim Trail Map 2, Section 7.

Best Seasons—Do this hike in early spring or later in the fall. After a mild winter, you can hike it from April through December.

Highlights—Emerald Bay provides many great hiking opportunities. On the edge of a beautiful sandy beach at the western edge of the bay is the Vikingsholm Castle with its granite touches, carved wood spikes and gargoyles, roof covered with wildflowers, and its gorgeous stained-glass windows. The castle was constructed in 1928-1929 by Mrs. Lora Knight, after she had purchased 239 acres at the end of Emerald Bay for $250,000. Trails lead from the Vikingsholm to a beautiful waterfall, and along both sides of Emerald Bay.

Heads Up!—During the summer, these trails (especially the 1-mile portion from the parking lot to the Vikingsholm) can be very busy! The best time to go is on a weekday in early spring or late fall, when you are more likely to have the place to yourself.

Getting There—From Tahoe City, drive 17 miles south on Highway 89 to the Vikingsholm parking lot located on the south side of the road (10 miles north of the intersection of Highway 50 and Highway 89 in South Lake Tahoe). During the summer, this lot can be full early in the day. An alternative parking area is located one-quarter mile farther south on Highway 89 at the Eagle Falls Trailhead. There is a fee to use either lot.

Brief Trail Description—The trail from the parking lot to the Vikingsholm is a gentle descent for a mile. Two trails lead out from the Vikingsholm. The first takes you 1.5 miles along the north side of Emerald Bay, in and out of sandy inlets, past the Emerald Bay Boat Campground, to Emerald Point. This south-facing section of trail is the first area to emerge from the winter snows. From Emerald Point, the trail continues across a small peninsula and heads north for 3 miles along the lakeshore to Bliss State Park (along the way keep your eyes open for ospreys and eagles).

A second trail leaves the Vikingsholm, and heads southwest a short distance to a junction at a bridge across Eagle Creek. A right turn will lead you up to Eagle Falls in a third of a mile. The falls are quite dramatic when filled with springtime runoff. If you make a left turn, you will cross Eagle Creek and travel past the Emerald Bay landslide of 1955, then along the southern side of the bay to Emerald Bay Campground, 1.5 miles from the Vikingsholm.

Loch Leven Lakes

Loch Leven Lakes

Difficulty—It is a moderately difficult, but well-graded climb to the first of the three Loch Leven Lakes. The journey between the lakes is an easy ascent. If you visit all the lakes and return, it is a total distance of a little less than 8 miles.

Best Seasons—Late-June to late October. The trail is at a relatively low elevation (5880 feet), but faces north in an area that receives much snow.

Highlights—This hike is 30 miles closer to the Bay Area and Sacramento than most other Sierra hikes. It is also easily accessible via Interstate 80. In just a few miles you can reach three wonderful lakes lying on granite benches. The two farthest lakes provide good camping opportunities and excellent swimming in relatively warm water. These lakes make especially attractive locations for family camping trips, since they are great to explore and easy enough to get to for many families.

Heads Up!—The easy accessibility of this trail make Loch Leven Lakes busy places throughout the summer. You will almost certainly not have the lakes to yourself.

Getting There—Take Interstate 80 to the Big Bend Exit, which is 1.5 miles east of Cisco Grove, and 6 miles west of Soda Springs. Drive about 1 mile south on Hampshire Rocks Road (Old Highway 40), past the Rainbow Lodge, and park on the right at the trailhead parking lot. It has a pit toilet and parking space for about ten vehicles.

Brief Trail Description—The trail is a pleasant woodsy walk up past several streams bordered by wildflowers, before it crosses a railroad track. At that point, it begins a moderate, well-graded climb through a thick forest of firs and pines. In just under 3 miles from the trailhead, you reach Upper Loch Leven Lake, followed in 0.3 mile by Middle Loch Leven Lake, and then at 3.9 miles from the trailhead, my favorite of the three, High Loch Leven Lake. Also nearby is Salmon Lake, accessed via a trail near the lowest lake. It is also shallow and warm and may be filled with catfish.

Winnemucca Lake/Round Top Lake

Difficulty—Easy to moderately difficult. This is a fairly short hike, only 2.5 miles to Winnemucca Lake and 3.4 miles to Round Top Lake, with a round-trip distance of 6.8 miles. The high elevation of this trail may make it moderately difficult for those not accustomed to high altitudes. The trail starts at 8590 feet with Round Top Lake sitting at 9350 feet elevation. A faint trail also leads from Round Top Lake up a very steep mile to the top of Round Top (10,381 feet). If you add Round Top to your itinerary, this hike is strenuous.

Best Seasons—Late-July through October. This hike is in a high elevation area that receives a tremendous amount of snow that can last till midsummer.

Highlights—If you are looking for relatively easy access to some tremendous high mountain scenery, this is a great choice. An incredible variety of wildflowers can be viewed between Carson Pass and Winnemucca Lake from late July through August. The prolific flower display may include lupine, elephant head, gentian, delphinium, monkeyflower, tiger lily, columbine, rein orchid, and a full palate of different colored paintbrush. The area around Round Top lake and mountain has a rugged appeal, and is a popular destination for summertime skiers and snowboarders, trying to find that last patch of snow. This hike is a good choice for those in the South Lake Tahoe area, only about 25 miles away.

Heads Up!—Permits are required to camp in the Mokelumne Wilderness Area, where much of this hike takes place. During the summer, permits can be obtained at the trailhead at Carson Pass. During the rest of the year, you need to contact the Amador Ranger District in Jackson, California at (209) 295-4251. Given the short distance to the lakes, and the fragility of this high-altitude location, it is best to dayhike this trail.

Getting There—The trail starts from Carson Pass near Kirkwood Ski Area south of Lake Tahoe. From Meyers, take Highway 89 south about 11 miles to the intersection of Highway 88 and 89 (Picketts Junction). Be sure to come to a complete stop at this remote intersection as the California Highway Patrol watches it closely. Turn right on Highway 88 and go approximately 9 miles through Hope Valley and up to Carson Pass. A parking area is on your left just as the road reaches the summit. An information center is at the trailhead (summers only).

Brief Trail Description—From the Carson Pass parking lot, your route is a gentle-to-moderate ascent for 2.5 miles to Winnemucca Lake. You will pass incredible summertime wildflower displays in the open areas below Winnemucca Lake. A mile farther of moderate climbing brings you to Round Top Lake, which sits in a basin just below huge rocky crags and Round Top (10,381 feet). From here you can follow a faint very steep trail to the top of Round Top, where you will find 360-degree, awe-inspiring views. Your views to the north include Lake Tahoe, and a number of high peaks surrounding it, including Freel Peak (10,881 feet), Mt. Tallac (9735 feet), Pyramid Peak (9983 feet) and on a clear day, Mt. Rose (10,776 feet), some 46 miles away. The last few hundred feet at the top of the mountain is steep, crumbly volcanic rock. Stop where the ridgetop trail meets the steep rock, for equally spectacular views without the added danger.

Crag Lake

Difficulty—Easy to moderately difficult.

Map—Tahoe Rim Trail Map 2, Section 7.

Best Seasons—Mid-June to mid-October. This trail provides late spring access to eastern Desolation Wilderness.

Highlights—Crag Lake is an especially magnificent spot with the high granite slab of Crag Peak looming over the lake. This hike is the easiest route into Desolation Wilderness from the Tahoe basin, and it usually is snow free a month earlier than Eagle Falls, Bay View, and Echo Lake, the other Tahoe area trailheads used to access Desolation Wilderness. Both lakes are great locations for swimming or camping.

Heads Up!—This trail is quite popular for both day-hiking and camping so parking can be limited in the summer. A permit is

Crag Lake and Peak

required to enter Desolation Wilderness. Day permits can be obtained at the trailhead, for backpacking permits contact the Forest Service office in South Lake Tahoe at (530) 573-2694.

Getting There—From Tahoe City, drive 10 miles south on Highway 89 to Meeks Bay (this is about 17 miles north of the intersection of Highway 50 and Highway 89 at the South Lake Tahoe "Y"). The trailhead is on the west side of Highway 89 at the bend in the road.

Brief Trail Description—This trail starts out as a level walk through widely scattered forest and a wildflower-dotted meadow, and then heads up into the trees following the path of Meeks Creek. In 4.6 miles you reach Genevieve Lake, and Crag Lake shortly thereafter. If you would like to hike farther, you can continue past Stony Ridge Lake and Rubicon Lake, before heading over Phipps Pass to the Tahoe Rim Trail and Middle Velma Lake. From Middle Velma Lake, Emerald Bay is just 5 miles away, making a spectacular 18 mile point-to-point hike.

Fontanillis/Velma Loop

Difficulty—Strenuous, 12-mile loop with 2000 feet of elevation gain.

Map—Tahoe Rim Trail Map 2, Section 7.

Best Seasons—Mid-July to early October

Highlights—Here is Desolation Wilderness in all its splendor, with spectacular views of granite peaks, mountain lakes and a variety of plant life. Eagle, Granite, Fontanillis, and Dicks lakes, as well as all three Velma Lakes, are excellent for swimming or camping.

Heads Up!—These trails, especially on the first mile to Eagle Lake, can be crowded in the summer. Day use and backpacking permits are required. Day-use permits can be obtained at the trailhead. To get a backpacking permit contact the Forest Service office at (530) 573-2694.

Getting There—You can start from either of two trailheads, both are located at the western end of Emerald Bay on Highway 89. The Eagle Lake/Eagle Falls trailhead is about 200 yards south of the Vikingsholm parking lot, which is about 17 miles south of Tahoe City, and 10 miles north of South Lake Tahoe. There is a fee for parking. The Bay View campground/trailhead is 1 mile south of the Eagle Falls trailhead on Highway 89, across from the vista parking area. Drive through the campground to its western edge where you will find trailhead parking.

Brief Trail Description—The Eagle Lake trail ascends about 1 mile to often crowded Eagle Lake. Then you stay left and climb steadily, and sometimes steeply, along the slope of south Maggies Peak to a junction 2.6 miles from the trailhead. If you are starting from the Bay View trailhead, you hike about 0.5 mile to a stunning view of Emerald Bay, and then another half mile to Granite Lake. Next is a steep set of switchbacks into the cleavage between Maggies Peaks (these breast-shaped mountains, also known as Round Buttons, were named after Maggie's breasts. Who was Maggie? Legend has it that she was a buxom barmaid at the Tahoe Tavern Resort in the late 1800s). Your Bay View trail reaches the saddle between the two peaks then descends to a junction, and a meeting with the Eagle Lake trail. From here, with both trails as one, you hike along rolling rocky terrain for a little less than a mile to a junction, where you take a left turn onto the trail leading to Dicks Lake. Now in the heart of the stark Desolation Wilderness, land of granite boulders, sandy soils and scattered trees, you go about 0.5 mile to a beautiful pond. This shallow body of water is a good swimming spot, and is especially pretty in the fall when the mountain heather which surrounds the lake turns bright red. Your journey ascends across a granite slab to a saddle and junction. A left turn climbs up to Dicks Pass, and a right turn takes you to Dicks and Fontanillis Lakes. You are now on the Tahoe Rim Trail/Pacific Crest Trail (For more detailed information on the next 2 miles of trail refer to the Tahoe Rim Trail description in Chapter 6). In 0.2 mile you meet another junction, with a left turn going to Dicks Lake in 100 yards, and a right turn heading to Fontanillis, your next destination. At Dicks Lake, look for osprey diving for fish in the evening. The trail follows along Fontanillis Lake and finally reaches its outlet creek.

The trail crosses the creek and heads downhill for about a mile along a ridge line to a junction. If you turn left, you will be heading to Middle Velma Lake on the Pacific Crest Trail/Tahoe Rim Trail. However, you should turn right, leave the TRT/PCT, and head uphill for a little over a mile back to the Dicks Lake junction, and then retrace your steps back to the Bay View/Eagle Falls trail junction. Hopefully, you left a car at both trailheads, which will enable you to hike a loop back to Emerald Bay via a different trail than where you began.

Donner to Squaw Valley

Difficulty—A strenuous hike of about 15 miles.

Best Seasons—Mid-July to mid-October. Patches of snow can last until August on the north-facing slope of Anderson Peak.

Highlights—This section of the Pacific Crest Trail provides miles of stunning 360-degree views from atop a windswept ridge. Ridgecrest views reach all the way from Mt. Rose in the northeast, to Lake Tahoe, in the southeast, with the Granite Chief Wilderness to the south and west. You will see a wide variety of terrain and wildflower species, including large fields of mule ears. This well-constructed trail has firm-packed sandy soils good for fast-moving, long-distance hikers or runners. All will enjoy its high-altitude remoteness. When Desolation Wilderness is packed with people, you may only encounter a few people on this trail. The trail goes by Roller Pass, a portion of the original Emigrant Trail used by pioneers when they came to California.

Heads Up!—Very little water is available on the trail, and if hiking in late summer or fall, assume that there will be no water. Early in the summer, a northeast-facing 100-foot-long section of trail about 3 miles into the trail may be treacherous if it is still covered with snow. Most of the trail is treeless and exposed to the sun and wind; be sure to bring plenty of sunscreen and a windbreaker. Your trail intersects with a variety of use paths descending from Shirley Canyon in the last mile of your route. Take care to avoid getting lost.

Getting There—Take Interstate 80 to the Soda Springs exit and drive 4 miles east on Highway 40 to Donner Summit (Sugar Bowl Academy will be on your right). Take a right turn at the summit, just before the road starts to go downhill, and go 0.2 mile to the trailhead on your left. This point-to-point hike requires a shuttle: be sure to leave a vehicle in Squaw Valley.

Brief Trail Description—Climb south on the Pacific Crest Trail, where in 1 mile you reach a junction with the Mt. Judah Loop trail. This alternate route heads up to Mt. Judah, which has excellent views, and then circles back and meets the PCT, adding 0.4 mile to your hike's length. About 2 miles into the hike you reach a saddle, Roller Pass. Just off the trail to the southeast, the Donner Party of 1846 winched their wagons up the steep slope below. Another 0.3 mile of gentle climbing brings you to another saddle below Mt. Lincoln. From here, the trail traverses across a steep slope, and then follows the ridgecrest with views in all directions for several miles to Anderson Peak. Your trail circles Anderson Peak, than climbs another ridge for a 1-mile journey to Tinker Knob, where a short use trail takes you to its summit.

At 8 miles into your hike, the trail now descends from Tinker Knob into a deep wide bowl (North Fork of American River Canyon) with wildflowers and sparse tree cover. You cross this bowl and then begin a steady climb, and at 4 miles from Tinker Knob, you reach a junction. Head east (left) on a steady downhill for 3 miles into Squaw Valley, where you will end the trail next to the Squaw Valley Fire Station.

Aloha Lake Loop via Tamarack Trail

Difficulty—This 12-mile loop is strenuous overall. The first 2.5 miles are very strenuous.

Map—Tahoe Rim Trail Map 1, Section 7.

Best Seasons—Mid-July through Mid-October.

Highlights—This is a classic hike into the heart of Desolation Wilderness with views of over a dozen lakes, numerous high granite and volcanic peaks, and a tremendous variety of mountain terrain.

Heads Up!—The first few miles up a canyon to a saddle are very steep, with almost 2000 feet of elevation gain. While not mountain climbing, it is certainly one of the steepest sections of trail I have ever hiked. It is especially difficult if you are carrying a heavy backpack. In the early summer this steep section can be icy and will require extra caution.

Getting There—Go about 0.5 mile west of Camp Richardson on Highway 89 and turn south on Fallen Leaf Lake Road (this is about 3 miles northwest of the intersection of Highway 50 and 89 in South Lake Tahoe). Follow this road 5.3 miles along the edge of Fallen Leaf Lake to the Glen Alpine Trailhead. The first 4.5 miles of the route are one and one-half lanes wide, and the last 0.8 miles is only one lane wide. From the Glen Alpine parking area, walk on Fallen Leaf Lake Road back toward the lake about 0.25 mile to the Tamarack trail on the right-hand (south) side.

Brief Trail Description—Hike 2.5 steep miles to a level junction with the Triangle Lake trail. These first few miles are extremely beautiful. You will hike through lush, almost jungle-like stream crossings with tiger lilies and columbines, and then climb through open areas of granite boulders from which you can enjoy great views. From the Triangle Lake junction go straight and climb more gently now to an open, almost treeless, viewpoint that faces Echo Lakes and Ralston Peak. Then, proceed downhill to a junction where the Tahoe Rim Trail/Pacific Crest Trail climbs up from Echo Lakes. Turn right on the PCT/TRT and follow the signs to Lake Aloha. For a more detailed description of the next 6 miles of trail along the Tahoe Rim Trail, refer to Section 7.

When you reach Lake Aloha, turn right, and head north along Aloha's eastern shore to a junction at its northern edge, where you turn right. In the next 2 miles you descend past two beautiful lakes, Heather and Susie. From Susie Lake you hike about 0.5 mile to a junction where you turn right. Now leaving the PCT/TRT you hike 0.5 mile to another junction, turn right, and follow it

3.3 miles, mostly downhill, to the Glen Alpine Trailhead where your car is parked.

Mountain Biking

Page Meadows/Ward Canyon

Difficulty—This area has a whole system of interconnected trails, which vary from easy to strenuous.

Map—Tahoe Rim Trail Map, Section 8.

Best Seasons—Late-June through late October. Do not ride through the meadows when they are wet.

Highlights—These trails have it all: rolling forested terrain, lush green meadows in the summer, and glorious yellow and red leaves in the fall. It is a fun, smooth single-track trail with good climbs and thrilling descents. The variety of trails encourages you to visit again and again.

Heads Up!—The meadow areas are fragile when wet and should be avoided. Sometimes the elaborate trail network can be confusing. You may end up coming out somewhere different than you think, but that's part of the fun.

Getting There—Five different locations can be used to access this great network of dirt roads and single-track trails.

1. Granlibakken Road: Go 0.5 mile south of Tahoe City on Highway 89, turn right on Granlibakken Road, then left on Rawhide which you take to its end. The trail starts behind a gate.
2. End of Silvertip in Talmont Estates: Take Highway 89 2 miles south of Tahoe City and turn right on Pine Street.

Mountain bikers on the East Shore

Then turn right on Tahoe Park Heights, right on Big Pine, and left on Silvertip, which you follow to its end.

3. Ward Canyon Boulevard: Go south from Tahoe City about 2.5 miles on Highway 89. Turn right on Pineland Drive. At the end of the straightaway, veer left and follow the "Ward Canyon" sign. Go about 1 mile and take the dirt road on your right side that you will see continuing on past a gate.

4. Chamonix: Follow the directions to #3 above, and go an additional mile on Ward Canyon Boulevard, which becomes Courchevel. Turn right on Chamonix and go to the end of the road where a trail heads west.

5. Snowcrest Road, Alpine Meadows: Take Highway 89 3.5 miles north from Tahoe City to Alpine Meadows Road, where you turn left. Go about 1 mile and turn left on Snowcrest. Follow this road to a gated dirt road on your left.

Brief Trail Description—With so many different entrances and a complicated network of trails, exact directions are not offered here. A number of looping trails exist that go around Page Meadows, up to the top of Scott Peak at Alpine Meadows, or into the Tahoe City/Rawhide Area. One loop starts at Rawhide, goes over to Snowcrest and then back along the bike trail between Alpine Meadows and Tahoe City. Another trail starts at Chamonix and goes around the meadows, then loops back to the same starting point, or down to Ward Canyon Boulevard. Explore the area and see where you end up.

Tahoe Cross Country Ski Area/Burton Creek State Park

Difficulty—Moderate. A variety of trails and loops provide opportunities for all riders from beginners to expert.

Map—Tahoe Rim Trail Map, Section 1.

Best Seasons—Late-June through November, or up to the first major snow. After mild winters with less than average snow, it is possible to access this area by late May.

Highlights—A gently rolling open forest makes for great riding on smooth trails. You will find beautiful meadows and several excellent lakeviews at the top of the climbs.

Heads Up!—It's easy to get lost in the confusing trail pattern here. This is a busy area so watch out for hikers, dogs, children, horses and bears.

Getting There—From Tahoe City, take Highway 28 about 2.5 miles northeast to Fabian Way and turn left. Turn right on Village and proceed to the top of the hill, where Village veers right. Quickly turn left on Country Club Drive, and left again into the Tahoe Cross Country ski area parking lot.

Brief Trail Description—From the Nordic center, go up the dirt road heading west. This area has dozens of miles of trails that go to Tahoe City, Truckee, Northstar, or Brockway Summit. Mt. Watson is located at about 8 miles of steady climbing from the Nordic center where you'll have great lakeviews. Most trails are easy to moderate and very fun to ride. The opportunities for different rides are almost endless. For a detailed description of the Tahoe Rim Trail portion of this trail system, refer to the trail description for Section 1.

Flume Trail/Tahoe Rim Trail loop

Difficulty—Strenuous. 23 mile round-trip with a lot of climbing. The Flume Trail portion, which is 4.5 miles long, is on the edge of a cliff and may give the agrophobically challenged the "heebee jeebees."

Map—Tahoe Rim Trail Map, Section 3.

Best Seasons—Mid-June through October.

Highlights—This is one of the most spectacular mountain biking routes in the United States. The views of Lake Tahoe are awe-inspiring, the fall colors can be extraordinary, and most of the trail is smooth and a treat to ride.

Heads Up!—This very popular trail is used by both hikers and bikers, and can be quite congested on weekends. Be especially cautious of hikers and follow the posted bike speed limits. The 4.5 mile Flume Trail portion of the trail, while well constructed, may be challenging to those who fear heights.

Getting There—Our trailhead is off of Highway 28, about 0.5 mile from the intersection of Highway 28 and Highway 50. It is located in the Lake Tahoe Nevada State Park at Spooner Lake, about 27 miles from Tahoe City and 14 miles from South Lake Tahoe. A fee is required to park, with the proceeds going to maintain the trails.

Brief Trail Description—From the parking lot, head down a short hill to North Canyon Road, which you follow about 4 miles uphill to the saddle above Marlette Lake. You will find maps placed at several kiosks along the route. A 1-mile descent takes you to a junction next to Marlette Lake. Turn left and follow the road around the west side of the lake to Marlette Lake's dam. To the left of the dam, the Flume Trail begins as a steep single track which quickly crosses the lake's outlet creek. For the next 4.5 miles the trail traverses, mostly level, over the location of the former water flume that ran from Marlette Lake to Carson City. This flume carried logs in the late 1800s to build Virginia City silver mines. The lakeviews from the Flume Trail are spectacular. Eventually the trail reaches Tunnel Creek Road.

If you would like a shorter ride, turn left and head down this road to Highway 28. In the summertime you can pay for a shuttle back to your car. Call (775) 749-5349 or go to www.theflumetrail. com for shuttle information and times.

To continue on the Flume Trail/TRT loop, turn right and head up the steep hill 0.5 mile to the Tahoe Rim Trail, where you turn right. Follow the trail past Twin Lakes and begin climbing. The TRT heads mostly uphill for 2.4 miles, and then mostly downhill for 2.7 miles to a junction at Hobart Road. Turn right on Hobart Road and soon you will head downhill steeply to your junction next to Marlette Lake. Now you are retracing your route to the saddle above Marlette Lake and then on a long, fun downhill on North Canyon Road back to the trailhead.

Commemorative Emigrant Trail

Difficulty—Easy to moderately difficult. For most people who have experience on single-track trails, this is a fun and not-too-difficult ride. It is a special treat for advanced riders looking for an opportunity to ride fast.

Best Seasons—Late-May to November. The snow is usually melted off this trail earlier than any other single-track trail in the North Tahoe/Truckee area. After a mild winter you may be able to ride this trail by mid-April.

Highlights—This is a fun ride with gentle ascents and descents through an open forest that can be completed by strong riders in about 2 hours. While the scattered forest scenery on this trail is pleasant, the great riding conditions are what make it especially enjoyable. Keep your eyes open for deer, commonly found along this trail.

Heads Up!—Since in the spring this may be the only North Tahoe area mountain biking trail free from snow, it can be over-crowded, especially on weekends. As the snow melts and other trails become available, the number of riders on this trail will drop significantly. In the middle of the summer this very exposed and dry trail can be quite hot and dusty.

Getting There—Take Highway 89 about 4 miles north from the intersection of Interstate 80 and Highway 89 in Truckee. Just as you bridge Prosser Creek (the first large creek you pass heading north from Truckee), you will see a dirt parking area on the right side. Your trail starts here.

Brief Description—The trail heads 9 miles north through a recently logged forest, eventually reaching Stampede Reservoir, where you turn around and return the same way. The trail intersects with many dirt roads, but just follow the well-labeled single-track trail. Along the route you will see several meadows and Mt. Rose in the distance through the trees.

8 Resources and Amenities

Listed below are public agencies, Forest Service information centers, and other useful tidbits to help you plan your trip to the Tahoe Rim Trail.

National Forest, Lake Tahoe Basin Management Unit
35 College Drive
South Lake Tahoe, CA 96150
(530) 543-2600
www.fs.fed.us/r5/ltbmu

National Forest, El Dorado National Forest Information Center
3070 Camino Heights Drive
Camino, CA 95709
(530) 644-6048
www.r5.fs.fed.us/eldorado

National Forest, Humboldt-Toiyabe National Forest
1536 South Carson Street
Carson City, NV 89701
(775) 882-2766
www.fs.fed.us/htnf

Sugar Pine, Emerald Bay and Mt. Tallac

National Forest, Tahoe National Forest
10342 Highway 89, North
Truckee, CA 96161
(530) 587-3558
www.r5.fs.fed.us/tahoe

Lake Tahoe Nevada State Park
P.O. Box 8867
Incline Village, NV 89452
(775) 831-0494
www.state.nv.us/stparks/lt

Tahoe Rim Trail Association
DWR Community Non-Profit Center
948 Incline Way
Incline Village, NV 89451
(775) 298-0012
info@tahoerimtrail.org / www.tahoerimtrail.org

Tom Harrison Maps
2 Falmouth Cove
San Rafael, CA 94901
(415) 456-7940
www.tomharrisonmaps.com

Useful Phone Numbers and Websites

Emergency	911
Tahoe Nordic Search and Rescue	(530) 581-4038
Placer County Sheriff	(530) 581-6300
El Dorado County Sheriff	(530) 573-3000
Nevada County Sheriff	(530) 582-7838
Washoe County Sheriff	(775) 832-4107

www.TahoeRimTrail.org
Official website of the Tahoe Rim Trail Association.

www.writeonrex.com
Author's website on hiking, biking, mountain biking, cross-country skiing, and writing.

www.Tahoetrips.com
Information on guided excursions at Lake Tahoe.

www.Tahoeguide.com
General guide for a variety of Tahoe information.

www.Tahoe.com
An all-purpose website that includes the local newspapers.

www.flyline.com
Information on fishing in the Sierra Nevada.

www.moonshineink.com
Truckee/Tahoe's great monthly newsmagazine.

www.tahoexc.org
Tahoe Cross Country Ski Area website.

www.spoonerlake.com
Spooner Lake Cross Country website.

www.theflumetrail.com
Flume Trail shuttle/Spooner Wilderness cabins information.

www.kirkwood.com
Information on Kirkwood Downhill and Cross-Country ski areas.

www.tahoemtnmilers.org/trt50
The site for information on Tahoe Rim Trail endurance runs.

http://tahoe.usgs.gov
Your scientific portal to Lake Tahoe information.

Afterword

Telling everyone about what the Tahoe Rim Trail has to offer is a joy to me. It is very satisfying to help others experience an incredible ridgetop view or the thrill of flying down a fun section of single-track trail. When I am guiding a trip and explaining about the beauty around us, it is invigorating and restorative. That said, when I go out for a mountain bike ride on one of my favorite sections of trail, I get a bit irritated to see all those other people out there as well. Who are all these people and why are they riding on this great trail that I used to have to myself? In writing this book, am I part of the problem? Am I fouling my own nest and the nest of others by telling everyone about the best places to go? Perhaps.

I hope that by providing the tools for people to enjoy their natural surroundings, I am increasing the understanding of how important it is that we protect the natural world. If you enjoyed this book and found it useful, please return the favor by doing what you can to protect what we still have and help restore what has been damaged or destroyed. Go to work maintaining a trail. Join the Tahoe Rim Trail, Sierra Club, or League to Save Lake Tahoe in an effort to keep this beautiful place as beautiful as it is now.

Another beautiful day begins at Lake Tahoe.

APPENDIX A

Mileages for the Tahoe Rim Trail

The mileages for the distances between points along the Tahoe Rim Trail are presented below. They are based on the cartographical work of the Tahoe Rim Trail Association, Jeffrey P. Schaffer, and Tom Harrison Maps.

Section Mileage Chart

Section Number	Location	Total Miles	Miles Between Points
Section 1	Tahoe City to Brockway Summit	19.2	
	Lava Rocks Viewpoint		3.4
	Cinder Cone		4.1
	Painted Rock		7.0
	Watson Lake		12.5
	Brockway Summit		19.2
Section 2	Brockway Summit to Tahoe Meadows Via Waterfall trail	19.6	
	Spur Trail to Viewpoint (Viewpoint, 1.5)		1.2
	Road to Martis Peak		4.3
	Rock Pile Viewpoint		6.8
	Wilderness Boundary		7.6
	Rose Knob Peak/Gray Lake Junction		9.8
	Gray Lake Junction/Mud Lake		11.2
	Relay Peak		14.6
	Radio Tower		15.0
	Mt. Rose Trail Junction		16.4
	Mt. Rose Highway		19.6

Section Number	Location	Total Miles	Miles Between Points
Section 3	Tahoe Meadows to Spooner Summit	23.1	
	Tunnel Creek Road		9.2
	Twin Lakes		9.5
	Christopher's Loop Junction (Viewpoint, 12.8)		11.6
	Marlette Peak Campground		13.8
	Hobart Road		14.3
	Marlette Lake via Hobart Road		16.4
	Spooner Lake via Hobart Road		21.2
	Snow Valley Peak Road		17.2
	Snow Valley Peak		17.5
	Spooner Summit Trailhead		23.1
Section 4	Spooner to Kingsbury	13.0	
	South Camp Peak		6.0
	Genoa Peak		7.8
	Kingsbury North Trailhead		13.0
Section 5	Kingsbury to Big Meadow Trailhead	23.2	
	Mott Canyon Creek		3.6
	Monument Pass		5.1
	Star Lake		8.8
	Freel Peak Saddle		10.7
	Armstrong Pass		13.7
	Tucker Flat (Saxon Creek Trail)		18.8
	Grass Lake Junction		21.2
	Grass Lake Trailhead		21.8
	Big Meadow Trailhead		23.2

Section Number	Location	Total Miles	Miles Between Points
Section 6	Big Meadow Trailhead to Echo Lake	17.5	
	Big Meadow		0.7
	Dardanelles Lake Junction		2.0
	Dardanelles Lake		3.4
	Round Lake		2.6
	PCT/TRT Junction		4.9
	Showers Lake		7.0
	Sayles Canyon Trail		10.5
	Bryan Meadow		11.4
	Echo Summit		15.3
	Echo Lake		17.5
Section 7	Echo Lake to Barker Pass	32.5	
	Upper Echo Lake Water Taxi		2.5
	Tamarack Lake		3.6
	Lake Aloha		6.0
	Junction with Mosquito Pass Trail		7.4
	Heather Lake		7.9
	Susie Lake		9.0
	Glen Alpine Springs Trail Junction		9.7
	Gilmore Lake		10.7
	Dicks Pass		13.6
	Junction to Bayview Trail		15.3
	Dicks Lake		15.5
	Fontanillis Lake		16.0
	Middle Velma Lake		17.5
	Phipps Peak Trail Junction		23.1
	Richardson Lake		26.0
	Miller Lake Jeep Road		28.2
	Barker Pass		32.5

Section Number	Location	Total Miles	Miles Between Points
Section 8	Barker Pass to Tahoe City	16.7	
	Twin Peaks Trail Junction		4.8
	Twin Peaks on TRT		6.0
	Junction of TRT/Stanford Rock Trail		6.3
	Ward Creek Road		11.5
	Tahoe City		16.7

Clockwise Mileage Chart

Location	Total Mileage	Distance Between Points	Counter-clockwise Mileage
Tahoe City North Trailhead	0.0	19.2	169.4
Brockway Summit Trailhead	19.2	19.7	150.2
Mt. Rose Highway/ Tahoe Meadows	38.9	0.8	130.5
Tahoe Meadows Trailhead	39.7	23.1	129.7
Spooner North Trailhead	62.8	—	106.6
Spooner South Trailhead	62.8	13.0	106.6
Kingsbury North Trailhead	75.8	3.4	93.6
Kingsbury South Trailhead	79.2	23.2	90.2
Big Meadow Trailhead	102.4	15.3	67.0
Echo Summit Trailhead	117.7	2.2	51.7
Echo Lake Trailhead	119.9	32.5	49.5
Barker Pass Trailhead	152.4	16.7	17.0
Tahoe City South Trailhead	169.1	0.3	0.3
Tahoe City North Trailhead	169.4	—	0.0

APPENDIX B

Tim's Top 5 Best Places on the Trail

For Views

Dicks Pass (Section 7)—Since it is quite a climb to reach the top, you'll want to spend some time enjoying the breathtaking views of two huge watersheds and a dozen lakes.

Christopher's Loop (Sections 3 and 4)—Located about halfway between Tahoe Meadows and Spooner Summit at the end of a short spur trail, it is not easy to reach this viewpoint, but you are rewarded with a view of of the entire lake and surrounding mountains (Section 3). The other great, east-shore lake view is from South Camp Peak, halfway between Spooner Summit and Kingsbury Grade (Section 4).

Granite Chief Wilderness between Barker Pass and Twin Peaks (Section 8)—Just south of the Pacific Crest Trail junction near Twin Peaks, at the end of a long climb, you reach a great open ridge, where you enter Granite Chief Wilderness. Views into the big valley of that wilderness, and toward Desolation Wilderness and Lake Tahoe, are spectacular. It's a perfect lunch spot.

Relay Peak (Section 2)—The high point of this ridge in the Mt. Rose area is referred to as the "Million Dollar Mile" as it affords spectacular 360-degree views. On a clear day you can see the Sierra Buttes and Lassen Peak to your north.

Lake Aloha (Section 7)—On a midsummer day without much wind, while you lounge on a rock with one foot in the water, it's unbeatable to gaze up at the Crystal Range.

To Swim

Lake Aloha (Section 7)—Here is Lake Aloha again. What can I say? If you swim from island to island offshore when the water is warm, you will swear you have died and gone to heaven.

Middle Velma Lake (Section 7)—This is another great lake for swimming, with numerous islands just begging for you to jump in and swim to them. If you are northbound on the TRT, it will be over 80 miles before the next really good swimming lake (and that one is colder).

Truckee River/Lake Tahoe (Section 1 and Section 8 Intersection)—Even though you cross the river right in the middle of Tahoe City, jump in and float around; it feels great. If you're ready for a break, consider a leisurely raft down the Truckee River; contact Mountain Air Sports at (530) 583-5606 for more information. Also the Commons Beach on Lake Tahoe in the center of Tahoe City is about 0.25 mile east of the Truckee River on Highway 28. If one is hiking the Tahoe Rim Trail doesn't it make sense to swim in Lake Tahoe?

Star Lake (Section 5)—Due to its high elevation the lake can be extremely brisk (OK, bone-chilling cold), but the views are great and Star is the best lake along the east-shore trail. If you hit it when it is warm it makes for a great swim.

Showers Lake (Section 6)—There are these big, flat, granite rocks that go right down to the water's edge, which make for great swimming *au naturel.*

To Ride a Bike

Painted Rock (Section 1)—Between Tahoe City and Brockway Summit, 2 miles in either direction of Painted Rock, is the smoothest, most enjoyable single-track trail you will ever ride. Your easiest access is from Dollar Hill at the Tahoe Cross Country Ski Area.

Tunnel Creek Road to Marlette Lake (Section 3)—This portion of trail can be used as part of a loop with the Flume Trail. It includes some tough climbs, and some thrilling downhills with spectacular views. Get off your bike to hike up to the view from Herlan Peak (aka Christopher's Loop).

Page Meadows (Section 8)—The Page Meadows area, which has an extensive network of trails besides the Tahoe Rim Trail, offers some wonderful twists and turns on very ridable terrain. Stay out of the meadow itself until it dries up in the late summer or fall.

Spooner South to South Camp Peak (Section 4)—This section offers great riding over sandy terrain with tremendous views along the way. Either turn around at the peak and enjoy the downhill stretch, or continue on to Kingsbury for something a little more challenging and technical.

Tahoe Meadows to Tunnel Creek (Section Three)—Only available for use on "even" days of the month, this is probably the most popular mountain biking section on the TRT. After an initial climb, it is mostly downhill, with beautiful sandy conditions and great views. Some parts are pretty technical, but if you go on a summer weekend the most difficult challenge may be avoiding the crowds.

To Camp

Lake Aloha (Section 7)—Hundreds of great spots are available on this big lake. It will give you privacy when the smaller Desolation Wilderness lakes are crowded.

Velma/Fontanillis/Dicks lakes (Section 7)—All of these give you the full Desolation Wilderness experience, however crowded they become in midsummer. Very few campsites are available at Fontanillis.

Barker Pass (Section 8)—About 2.5 miles north of Barker Pass is a peaceful little meadow with great views, a stream, and a nice camping spot among the trees.

Star Lake (Section 5)—This lake is beautiful, the campsites have views of Tahoe as well as Star Lake, and the next lake is at least 17 miles away. Isn't it time to make camp? If you are feeling energetic you can hike up to the top of Freel Peak in the morning, only 2 miles away.

Showers Lake (Section 6)—Showers is a beautiful little lake offering great swimming and fine views. If you go there in the middle of the week, it might even be quiet and peaceful.

APPENDIX C
Ways to Save Lake Tahoe

We have been blessed with a deep blue alpine lake surrounded by majestic mountains. We must make an effort to preserve this lake and its environment so that future generations can enjoy it as well. The Tahoe Regional Planning Agency has come up with ways to save Lake Tahoe. A few of the best are listed below. These are a good place to start, but don't hesitate to think up your own.

1. Take the bus. Share a ride. Take a hike. Ride a bike. When you pick up your car keys, stop to plan the trip you're about to make. Can you run several errands while you're out? Could you save this trip until you need to make another? Is there another way you could get there? Reducing the number of trips you make and getting around without getting in your car reduces traffic congestion, helps protect excellent air quality, and may improve your social skills and your health.

2. Fill . . . don't spill. If you fill it to the brim, gasoline may spill out of your tank and into Lake Tahoe.

3. Skip a stone and leave the other rocks alone. Rocks of all sizes and shapes are fish habitat. Fish need rocks to carry out their life cycles. Underwater rock gardens are where they spawn, feed, and hide from predators. By moving or rearranging rocks you might destroy valuable habitat.

4. Don't be a trail blazer. Erosion from unmaintained dirt roads presents a serious water-quality challenge. Off-highway vehicles and dirt bikes contribute to erosion when they travel off the maintained roads. Kids, stay on the designated roads. Parents, make sure your kids stay on the designated roads.

5. Take the beaten path. The tread from hiking boots and mountain-bike tires are enough to cause erosion in the back country, so it's best to stay on the trail.

6. You can lead a horse to water, but you shouldn't set up camp there. The less activity there is in a stream environment zone, the better. The law requires that you pitch your tent no less than 200 feet from a body of water. That includes lakes, streams, creeks, reservoirs, and rivers.

7. Garbage in/garbage out. You could even pick up after a litterbug who went before you.

8. Finally, teach your children well.

The above information was provided as a courtesy of the Tahoe Regional Planning Agency. For more information, call them at (775) 588-4547.

Index

For specific place names, trails and roads, see "Index to Place Names," and "Index to Trails and Roads" below.

About the Author

Tim Hauserman has been a resident of North Lake Tahoe since 1960. He has hiked and biked in the area for many years and has been a guide for the Sierra Club, Tahoe Trips and Trails (a private excursion company), and the Tahoe Rim Trail. A member of the Tahoe Rim Trail Board of Directors from 1998-2007, he became the 11th member of the Tahoe Rim Trail 165-Mile Club in 1999. His other books include *Monsters in the Woods: Backpacking with Children,* and *Cross-Country Skiing in the Sierra Nevada*. He also writes for a variety of local and regional publications. Tim lives with his wife Sandy and two children, Sarah and Hannah, on the west shore of Lake Tahoe. He likes to hike, bike ride, cross-country ski, kayak, and practice yoga.

The Tahoe Rim Trail Association

The Tahoe Rim Trail celebrated its 25th anniversary at the Tahoe Meadows Trailhead in July 2007. "Much has happened in the past 25 years as this trail and organization grew from an idea and dream of one man into the dream and desire of thousands of supporters," said Steve Anderson, President of the TRTA Board of Directors. Also in 2007, *National Geographic Adventure Magazine* included the Tahoe Rim Trail in its list of top ten adventure vacations in the country. This was recognition not only of the trail's intrinsic recreational value and scenic beauty, but also of the thousands of hours of volunteer work expended to complete this project. More than 10,000 volunteers have worked nearly 200,000 hours to make the trail a reality, and it is considered one of the largest volunteer projects in the country. Even with the completion of the trail, the work is not finished. The TRTA anticipates many more years of maintenance to preserve this legacy. The organization is actively involved in trail and trailhead improvements, bridge construction, roadway-to-single-track improvements, creating a wide array of educational programs, and supporting the trail users that come from all over the world to explore this wonderful "trail like no other."

 For more information, visit the Tahoe Rim Trail Association website at www.tahoerimtrail.org.